No
More
Boring
Bible
Study

No More Boring Bible Study

WHY TAKING SCRIPTURE
SERIOUSLY IS EASIER AND MORE
EXCITING THAN YOU THINK

Faith Womack

ZONDERVAN BOOKS

ZONDERVAN BOOKS

No More Boring Bible Study
Copyright © 2025 by Faith J. Womack

Published by Zondervan, 3950 Sparks Drive SE, Suite 101, Grand Rapids, MI 49546, USA. Zondervan is a registered trademark of The Zondervan Corporation, L.L.C., a wholly owned subsidiary of HarperCollins Christian Publishing, Inc.

Requests for information should be addressed to customercare@harpercollins.com.

Zondervan titles may be purchased in bulk for educational, business, fundraising, or sales promotional use. For information, please email SpecialMarkets@Zondervan.com.

ISBN 978-0-310-36940-0 (audio)

Library of Congress Cataloging-in-Publication Data

Names: Womack, Faith, 1994- author
Title: No more boring Bible study : why taking scripture seriously is easier and more exciting than you think / Faith Womack.
Description: Grand Rapids, Michigan : Zondervan Books, [2025]
Identifiers: LCCN 2025025117 (print) | LCCN 2025025118 (ebook) | ISBN 9780310369370 trade paperback | ISBN 9780310369394 ebook
Subjects: LCSH: Bible—Study and teaching
Classification: LCC BS600.3 .W66 2025 (print) | LCC BS600.3 (ebook) | DDC 220.071—dc23/eng/20250813
LC record available at https://lccn.loc.gov/2025025117
LC ebook record available at https://lccn.loc.gov/2025025118

Published in association with The Bindery Agency, www.TheBinderyAgency.com.

HarperCollins Publishers, Macken House, 39/40 Mayor Street Upper, Dublin 1, D01 C9W8, Ireland (https://www.harpercollins.com)

Cover design: Lindy Kasler
Cover illustrations: Lindy Kasler / Shutterstock
Interior design: Kait Lamphere

Printed in the United States of America

26 27 28 29 30 LBC 11 10 9 8 7

For Joseph, the quiet strength in my chaos
Thank you for your steady, selfless love,
which I could never deserve. I love you
more than words could ever write.

And for Winchester and Sutton
You are the most beautiful boys the earth has
ever held. One day, you'll carry the gospel to the
far reaches of the world. Momma is so proud.

And to my uncle, Patrick Keane
You ran the race with quiet faithfulness. Thank you
for showing me what it looks like to finish well.

Contents

Preface

ᨆᨆᨆᨆᨆᨆᨆᨆᨆ

Wow, it was brave of you to pick up this book. Some people believe the Bible is a dead, old, boring book. But some of us believe there is more to God's Word, if we can just get into it.

The truth is we would never actually tell anyone we sometimes secretly believe the Bible is a bit boring. But we feel it in the depths of our soul. We've all been there—longing to do anything else but sit down and read Lamentations. Studying the Bible is not what we spend all day at the office dreaming about doing when we get home. It's just not as engaging as social media, and after a wild day at work we'd sometimes rather watch a reality show than read about a random king from 2 Chronicles.

So how do we avoid ignoring the Bible altogether? None of us want to be that Christian with the dusty Bible on their nightstand. There are lots of reasons we avoid Scripture, of course, but sometimes we neglect it because we simply don't understand its message, application, and power.

This book is written for the believers who want to actually understand their Bibles. And for anyone who is sick of feeling a little guilty about not liking to read the Bible. If that's you, then this book will likely transform your Bible studies forever, and I'm humbled to be a part of that transformation.

But first things first—I need to come clean with you. I have fallen in love with the Bible. I sit on the couch and try to watch a movie, and all I can think about is studying that one interesting verse in Philemon. Yes, it *is* possible for this kind of transformation to happen! I've found hundreds of thousands of other Christians online just like me; we identify ourselves as "Bible Nerds." And I've had the privilege of watching some of these people go from newbie Scripture readers to mature Bible Nerds.

Maybe you're not so sure about embracing a ridiculous label such as Bible Nerd, but you're going through intense trials in life and desperately want to know what God wants of you and how you can understand his Word and apply it to your life. Or maybe you've come to realize you've never truly read the Bible and you don't know where to start. Whatever your story is, I'm ready to come alongside you, and I'm filled with exhilarating joy because I know this journey will change the way you view the Bible forever. The message in this book is my anthem. I believe all Christians everywhere should know and understand Scripture. Within the pages of this book you will find wisdom from countless scholars who've gone before me, my own words and thoughts, and things I've learned in my own schooling and personal studies. In this age of information, as access to the Word of God has increased, the question now is how to read the Bible faithfully and enjoy studying it.

I believe you won't ever enjoy reading the Bible until you can understand it. You also won't understand it until you realize how it was intended to be read. In this book we will talk about what it means to read the Word of God as well as fall in love with it along the way. Because taking Scripture seriously—and being faithful to it—is easier and more exciting than you'd think!

But beware—you won't be the same Christian coming out of this book as you were going in. But that's just it. You're already here, reading. You're already learning and changing, and God has led—dare I say it?—*called* you to this venture.

CHAPTER 1

If We Truly Believe It's True

Tom Thumb isn't a noteworthy grocery store. The regional chain is sprinkled across Texas and carries much of the same stuff you'll find in your own grocery stores. Nearly everything about Tom Thumb is the same as in any other traditional grocery store I've been to. You could plaster "Kroger" or "Piggly Wiggly" across the front of the store and most people wouldn't know the difference because it's just that ordinary.

But when I hear "Tom Thumb," my chest gets heavy and my breath gets short. My eyes may get watery, and I will most likely change the subject or try to crack some kind of joke. The name alone makes me uncomfortable. That's because Tom Thumb is no ordinary grocery store to me. It carries some of my most painful memories. Grief is weird like that; it makes you hold on to the oddest things at the most random times, apparently for no particular reason. I don't know how to write this next part without it sounding cliché, but Tom Thumb is the place where I learned my parents were getting a divorce.

Yes, this whole book really does start in a Tom Thumb parking lot. Sixteen-year-old me unbuckled her seat belt, ready to exit the car, get out of the hot Texas sun, and start shopping in the air-conditioned grocery store. But my mom sighed, sat back in her seat, and laid out one of the hardest realities I didn't want to hear. She told me more than I wanted to know about her relationship with my dad, sharing things I already knew but wanted to ignore. After years of struggling, she explained, she was leaving my father.

My parents eventually went through a divorce that took three years to finalize. When my mom left my dad, I was so confused and hurt that I didn't know what to do—or what God would have me do. All my immature brain could comprehend was *Divorce is bad, and my mother is causing it.* So I chose to stay with my dad. After all, *she* was leaving *him*!

That left me under the care of my father, who informed me that God wanted him not to work. God also wanted him to "let" my mom leave him. God wanted him to stay in a house he couldn't afford after he lost his job. His reasoning? "Because Proverbs says this . . ." or "Because Proverbs says that . . ." As with any divorce, there were many underlying issues, one of which was serious scriptural abuse.

I was an immature Christian, so my dad's commitment to what he believed, and his strong sense of calling, seemed impressive and inspiring to me. He appealed to my heart's cry to feel like I mattered to God. After all, every young person's desire is to feel important. Dad told me things like "God is using you, in this house, for his plan." Sadly, what I didn't know was that my earthly father was using me as a pawn. Even more, he was mishandling the Word of God. I was being fed a dangerous combination of random scriptures taken out of context, as well as unbiblical, works-based, health-and-wealth theology, and I fell for it hook, line, and sinker.

For years I lived controlled by a man who *seemed* to be close to God. He seemed to know the Bible and he seemed to understand a lot of sermons.

He's just going through a tough season, I'd reassure myself when people questioned what he was telling me.

My father had lost his job and his wife, but he appeared to be focused on what God wanted from him—surely, he wasn't the bad guy. All the while he was doing things like "borrowing" my Christmas money for "business ventures." He quit paying our electricity bill and talked often about how the bank could kick us out of our home at any time, which left me in a constant state of fear and panic. The truth was that my father did not care for me, his wife, or God's Word. We were all pieces to manipulate in his twisted reality.

Meanwhile, as a high school student trying to grow in her faith under the guidance of her father—a self-appointed "spiritual mentor"—I didn't understand why God wasn't answering my prayers. I kept praying that my dad would get a job. I had all my friends at school praying for this too. What I couldn't see, however, was Dad's spiritual abuse and misuse of Scripture. Though I would like to believe it was all pure ignorance, his misuse of the Scriptures and constant refrain of "God told me" led him into countless bankruptcy filings. He ostracized himself from the church, disregarded anyone who tried to hold him accountable, and dismissed everyone who disagreed with his lifestyle. This meant he had no relationship with his ex-wife or his children.

Here's an example of the power of biblical interpretation. My father used Proverbs 11:4[1] to justify why he'd stopped paying his mortgage and then abused the Texas foreclosure system so he could stay in his house for years. He used another verse to justify why he was called by God not to work and instead draw unemployment benefits. Later on, when I went no contact with him, he used Exodus 20:12[2] against me, saying I was cursed to die young. I still remember where I was standing when I opened the letter from him that contained those words. My eyes glazed over as I read his handwriting on the page: "You're cursed." Those words didn't sit lightly with me. But it took a grand total of about three minutes to look up the reference for myself and see that my father was turning a blessing in Scripture into a curse. He was twisting God's Word for his benefit.

But the Lord used this heartbreak, confusion, and loss to light within me a fire to teach others how to read the Bible faithfully.

Hopefully, this story feels extreme to you. I pray you have not experienced anything like it in your life. Yet I know all too well that my family is not the only one affected by wrong interpretations of the Bible. I read stories every day about Christians leaving the church because of hurt and abuse. I hear countless horror stories of false teachers taking others' money and promising God's answer to prayer, leaving behind stadiums and megachurches full of exploited Christians.

---

1. "Wealth is worthless in the day of wrath, but righteousness delivers from death."

2. "Honor your father and your mother, so that you may live long in the land the LORD your God is giving you."

That is why I'm writing this book. It's for my younger, confused self and others like me. For the grandmother writing another check for another liar's private jet. But also for those who have been in the church all their lives but never discovered the beauty of the Word. We all deserve to taste the excitement and enjoyment of studying the Bible. And we all need to have clarity on what Scripture says.

During my parents' divorce, I was so confused about who was right and who was wrong. Both of them used Scripture to argue why they were right. How was I supposed to know what God wanted and why God's will seemed so confusing?

You probably have similar questions about biblical faith and its practical influence on life. Maybe you wonder why God allows evil. Why God feels distant. What he wants from you. I had those questions too. By God's grace, a few months after high school graduation I enrolled at Covenant College, a twelve-hour drive from my father, to pursue a degree in biblical and theological studies. I was eager and ready to study the Word and find answers to my questions, but I had no idea how quickly education would change everything for me.

Within one week of arriving on campus, the "lights" turned on. My third day on campus, I listened to a college orientation lecture that contradicted much of what my father had told me about Scripture. When I called Dad to discuss it, he told me he wanted nothing to do with the conversation. He had his mind set on what he wanted the Bible to mean to him. But for me the fire to learn had been lit. And I needed to know more.

Eventually I married my husband, whom I met at Covenant College and who was pursuing pastoral ministry. He went to seminary and began ministry as the Lord blessed us with two precious boys, Winchester and Sutton. I would inundate him with questions about his lectures and studies, and so eventually I, too, went on to complete a seminary degree, while caring for a toddler and an infant at home, because this fire had grown so large. No number of late nights nursing my son to sleep would stop me from studying the Word. As I sat in class lectures learning about the Bible, I kept having one lightbulb moment after another, and I thought, *All Christians need to know this stuff!*

This book is a compilation of all the things I wish I hadn't had to take out student loans to learn. These are the things I believe all Christians should know so that they can be faithful readers of Scripture.

We will discuss how to read the Bible, understand its literary genres, see the big picture, and apply its truth to our lives. This is what scholars call *hermeneutics*—the study of how we read and interpret the Bible. Hermeneutics is a guardrail that keeps us in line with what the text is actually saying in Exodus 20, for example, so that we don't misuse it and make it into a curse, like my dad did. Hermeneutics is what guides us as we listen to a sermon, helping us determine whether the preacher is being faithful to the text.

Hermeneutics is also what prevents us from hurting others and wrecking our own lives. This life is a gift and we are called to live for the Lord, so why spend even one second twisting his Word to say anything other than what it says? I don't know about you, but I want to live as though each day is precious. I don't want to waste a single day, month, or year neglecting what I believe is true. Because ultimately that's the issue here:

If we really believe that the Bible is true, we will want to be faithful to it, changed by it, and not misuse it.

So the question is this: Do you really believe the Bible is true?

Consider the Context

It's so easy not to consider whether we really believe the Bible is true. It's easy to say, "Yeah, yeah, yeah, Faith. I believe the Bible is true. Can we move on now?" But hermeneutics isn't just a game made up by scholars who wanted some rules. Hermeneutics isn't even a cheat code to the Bible. Hermeneutics (remember, this is the study of how to read the Bible so we can interpret the Bible) exists because the Bible is true. If it weren't true, it wouldn't really matter whether someone interpreted it differently from the author's meaning. But when it comes to the Bible, the use of hermeneutics is crucial for us to make sure we are understanding, believing, and following God as intended by his Word.

Take Philippians 4:13, for example. It's one of the most famous verses in the Bible. I've seen it on bumper stickers, on tattoos, and in nearly every Christian school's locker room. It sure is encouraging to read the words "I can do all things through Christ who strengthens me" before gym class as you lace up your shoes and prepare to run the mile. But this verse is often taken out of context. When he wrote it, Paul was not picturing my futile effort to get an A in gym class. In Philippians chapter 4, Paul is actually talking about God's provision in his life. Figure 1.1 shows Philippians 4:13 in context.

Philippians 4:10–19

The church is concerned for Paul. Why?

[10] I rejoiced greatly in the Lord that at last you renewed your concern for me. Indeed, you were concerned, but you had no opportunity to show it. [11] I am not saying this because I am in need, for I have learned to be content whatever the circumstances. [12] I know what it is to be in need, and I know what it is to have plenty. I have learned the secret of being content in any and every situation, whether well fed or hungry, y whether living in plenty or in want. [13] I can do all this through him who gives me strength.

Because he is in need! How bad is this need?

Oh, it doesn't matter how bad!

[14] Yet it was good of you to share in my troubles. [15] Moreover, as you Philippians know, in the early days of your acquaintance with the gospel, when I set out from Macedonia, not one church shared with me in the matter of giving and receiving, except you only; [16] for even when I was in Thessalonica, you sent me aid more than once when I was in need. [17] Not that I desire your gifts; what I desire is that more be credited to your account. [18] I have received full payment and have more than enough. I am amply supplied, now that I have received from Epaphroditus the gifts you sent. They are a fragrant offering, an acceptable sacrifice, pleasing to God. [19] And my God will meet all your needs according to the riches of his glory in Christ Jesus.

They gave to him in need! They cared for him!

TESTIMONY

From their generosity and his own lessons in contentment, he can attest that God is more than enough for us! His focus is to encourage them in the provision of God and the contentment of walking in the Spirit.

From the Philippians' generosity and his own lessons in contentment, Paul can attest that God is more than enough for us. Paul's focus is to encourage the Philippians in the provision of God and the contentment of walking in the Spirit. Paul is saying that God carried him through the lowest of the lows in prison—where he experienced beatings and starvation—and despite those situations he was able to be content in the Lord. He is saying he didn't have to be comfortable to be content in God. And he is saying he has all he desires in the Lord.

That meaning is much richer than "I can run the mile in

gym class through Christ who strengthens me." It is more than encouragement; it is assurance that even if I can't finish that run because my asthma kicks in and Coach gives me that terrible glare, I can be content because I have everything I need in Christ. This is the power of hermeneutics. Context can transform our understanding of the text, and when we neglect the context, we will often interpret a Bible verse to mean something it doesn't.

Are you starting to see the issue here? If we truly believe the Bible is true, we will want to be faithful to it and not misuse it. We will not plaster Philippians 4:13 on everything, because we now know we are taking it out of context or making it say something different from what Paul intended. We now know that what Paul was saying was significantly more encouraging and richer than some sort of me-centric platitude like "I can do all things." We realize that the comfort and value of Philippians 4:13 is found in the contextualized suffering of Paul and the provision of Christ in that suffering. It was never about running the mile in gym class, and while God does indeed care about every part of our lives, the good news is that it is so much bigger than just us.[3]

At this point you might be feeling a little frustrated that no one taught you about context sooner. At least, that's how I feel when I learn something new about reading the Bible. But, friend, it has never been about our doing enough or reading the Bible perfectly. We are saved not because we are enough but because we aren't.

---

3. I'm not saying you have to get that Philippians 4:13 tattoo removed or start a debate with someone over their use of the verse. True spiritual maturity and discernment is to know you can gain a proper grasp of the context of Philippians 4:13 but hurt a relationship through the process. Hermeneutics isn't some spiritual high ground or something to throw around like a social trump card. No, when we learn these nuggets of wisdom, it is our job to steward them appropriately in our lives first before we repaint the Christian school's locker room.

We aren't good enough. We mess up even the reading of Scripture. But praise God that he saved us as sinners, not because we are righteous in and of ourselves.[4] God saved us because we could never make ourselves worthy. So be comforted. There is grace. God doesn't make sure we have Israel's history memorized or that we've read the whole Bible before he wraps his saving arms around our hell-bound hearts. No, God saved us while we were still sinners—destitute, dying, and deeply in need of a Savior. So as we talk about the need to read the Bible more faithfully, remember that the grace of God is stronger than our sin and inadequacy.

Scripture is alive and active, sharper than any two-edged sword (Heb. 4:12). Scripture works even when it is misused. God isn't limited by our sin. But if we understand the power of truth, especially the good news of Jesus, how could we want to do anything less than be as faithful to it as possible? Just as Alcoholics Anonymous meetings begin with the verbal acknowledgment "Hi, my name is _____ and I am an alcoholic," I would love for us to start this book with a statement: "Hi, my name is Faith and I'm a recovering Bible twister." Doesn't have the same ring to it, does it? I'll keep brainstorming that.

Bible Nerd Notes

1. **RECAP.** Hermeneutics is the study of how we interpret the Bible, including the evaluation of how we read it. Reflect on some basic rules you use when you read different types of literature today.

---

4. Romans 5:8.

You probably read the Bible differently than you read bestselling books and school textbooks. Why is that? What do you know about the Bible that makes you read it differently?

2. **INVESTIGATE.** Context is everything—including the historical moment in which something is written and the content around a single Bible verse. Remember how discovering the context of Philippians 4 transformed our reading of "I can do all things"? This helps us to accurately interpret and apply Bible verses. When we ignore who wrote something and why they wrote it, it's easy to twist it to say anything we want it to say. This is why it is so important to consider everything in context. Consider taking notes in your Bible that mark the context and meaning of Philippians 4:13, then reread the chapter in your Bible. Does anything new stick out to you or convict you?

3. **REFLECT.** Think about why it is so important to be faithful to the Bible's intended meaning, whether God can still work through its misuse. Do we still believe it is true if we are willing to misuse it?

CHAPTER 2
CHAPTER 2

Is It True?

About a year ago I was mindlessly scrolling TikTok when a young teen seated atop her bed began to yell at me through the screen: "Guys! Grab your Bibles *right now*! Flip to this verse! Does your Bible have it? If not, throw it out *now*! You got a bad one!" Her face was red with terror, and she was clearly amazed at her findings. The comments were even worse: They all showed pure shock that their Bibles had a missing verse. No one knew anything about this "missing verse," and everyone was thanking her for her discovery.

My blood boiled as I thought about all the Sunday school teachers and pastors who had failed her. Sure, she was misinformed, but I understood how she'd gotten there. In many Bible versions, Matthew 17 skips from verse 20 to verse 22, with no verse 21. This TikTok creator had realized there was a missing verse and assumed it was cut out to hide the truth, when in fact it had been removed to preserve truth. It is not considered original but rather a later addition to the text.

Scholars widely accept that some Bible verses are not original to the earliest manuscripts.[1] That is why they have been removed from more recent publications. Remember, verse numbers are not original to the Bible; they were added in the sixteenth century. Once scholars found substantial proof that these verses (usually they are small side statements, never anything of substantial theology) were added later, they removed them. Now our Bibles may skip from verse 20 to verse 22, but that's for the preservation of truth. This TikTok influencer was effectively telling people to throw out the more accurate Bibles! Her video still haunts me to this day. I think about her horrified eyes. I remember the tight grip she had on her Bible, and I shudder when I think about the impact her video probably had on some viewers. So today, I hope to calm your fears and anxieties around the topic of translations as well as give you a few rules of thumb so that we trust our Bibles more, not less. And if we want to talk about trusting the Bible, we need to first learn a couple of vocabulary words and a little about Bible preservation and translation.

Rule of Thumb 1: Reliability

In biblical studies we have some big words we use when we're talking about the reliability of the Bible. A fancy word you might have heard before is *inerrancy*. This means that something is without error. Countless debates have centered on this concept. We know that some scribes copied the Bible down

---

1. Don't worry, these are not verses of significant theological meaning. Most the time they are transitional verses or stories of Jesus' character and grace that are similar to those in other accounts. For more on this, see Daniel B. Wallace, ed., *Revisiting the Corruption of the New Testament: Manuscript, Patristic, and Apocryphal Evidence* (Grand Rapids, MI: Kregel, 2011).

and accidentally left out a letter here and there. We know some translations have been corrected or refined over the years. So what does biblical inerrancy mean? It means the original document was perfect and without error. *Infallibility* is a similar word, and it means that the Bible is true in its purpose, message, and promises.[2] Despite the misspellings or the sleepy scribe who copied something wrong, the Bible's infallibility means it is trustworthy—it's not deceiving us in some way.

Some Christians walk away from the Bible because they fear how it might have been shaped through time and translations. But they don't want to reject Jesus. I discourage you from following this "take Jesus but leave the Bible" approach, because all our ideas about Jesus come from the Scriptures. If we cut out some parts and leave only what we like, then we are writing our own religion.

I have been reading and studying God's Word for years, and I've found that what we have today in our Bibles is surprisingly original and reliable. Common sense would tell us that over the course of two thousand years, written documents would evolve and change—significantly. But the Bibles we hold are shockingly similar to the oldest copies and manuscripts we have. There is an entire field of study called textual criticism, which looks at biblical manuscripts, parchments, and papyri to examine variants, or differences, in them. Scholars have done this type of study for hundreds of years, and they have created an in-depth rating system for the reliability of one variant over the other. We can hold up

---

2. Many scholars debate the extent of inerrancy, while others hold to infallibility but not inerrancy. For a helpful read on the spectrum of views on inerrancy, check out the debate between scholars exhibited in *Five Views on Biblical Inerrancy*, with contributions from R. Albert Mohler Jr., Peter Enns, Michael F. Bird, Kevin J. Vanhoozer, and John R. Franke.

papyri from the second and third centuries (within two hundred years of people who met Jesus here on earth) and compare them to our modern English translations, which are extremely close. We even have entire Bibles from the fourth and fifth centuries that scholars compare with earlier papyri, and it's amazing how consistent they are.[3] If you could read Greek, or any of these ancient languages, you'd find that our Bibles are translated faithfully—they have not really morphed or changed the message at all!

We stand on the shoulders of thousands of scholars who over the years have studied these manuscripts intensely and compiled the most faithful translations possible. The Bible is not something that has slowly evolved over time, like skeptics sometimes claim.[4] The reliability of each parchment is persistently revisited, scholars are frequently held accountable, and we all reap the benefits.

It is also important to note that the majority of variants in manuscripts have no theological influence on the basics of the gospel. The differences might be as simple as a misspelling or an ancient "typo." F. F. Bruce once said, "The variant readings about which any doubt remains among textual critics of the New Testament affect no material question of historic fact or

---

3. For more on this, check out the Codex Vaticanus, a manuscript of the Greek Bible, and Papyrus 75 (P75), an early Greek New Testament manuscript. Vaticanus is commonly understood to be from the fourth century but is closely aligned to the wordage in P75, from the third. Yet Vaticanus is not a copy of P75; textual critics know this by their differences. Rather, both go back to a very early tradition of careful copying in Alexandria.

4. Skeptics of the Bible, such as Bart D. Ehrman in *Misquoting Jesus: The Story Behind Who Changed the Bible and Why*, often claim that God's Word is unreliable. In *Revisiting the Corruption of the New Testament*, Wallace says, "The handwritten copies of the NT contain a lot of differences. We are not sure exactly what the number is, but the best estimate is somewhere between 300,000 and 400,000 variants. This means, as Ehrman is fond of saying, that there are more variants in the MSS than there are words in the NT. The vast bulk of these differences affect virtually nothing. We concur on the wording of the original text almost all the time" (20). The number of variants is debated and could be even more than that estimation, but this doesn't change the fact that what we have today is shockingly similar to what we find from long ago.

of Christian faith and practice."[5] The reality is that the Bible we have today is *too* reliable and trustworthy for us to let it get dusty on our nightstands. This document has changed human history, and we are still reading and studying it today because it is so much more than just an old book. It is too alive and too active for Christians to pretend like they don't need to read it. It is also too close to the most accurate manuscripts we've found to be anything but the Word of God.[6]

Reliability is rule of thumb 1 to our conversation around translations because there is too much false information swirling around online and in Christian circles. I've heard too many ill-informed Christians refer to a "bad" translation or even an "evil" translation. They don't realize that translations are tools that help us understand the same text, from the original languages. Arguably, the most popular translations, such as the NIV, ESV, NASB, NET, NLT, and RSV, are based on the closest English synonyms[7] of the original Greek, Hebrew, or Aramaic. And please note that popularity isn't the most important metric.[8] (For example, I'm excluding the Passion Translation and *The Message* because they're paraphrases.[9])

---

5. F. F. Bruce, *The New Testament Documents: Are They Reliable?* (Downers Grove, IL: InterVarsity Press, 1960), 19–20.

6. My friend Daniel B. Wallace has spent his life on this work. If you're interested in the topic of the reliability of Scripture, I encourage you to watch his numerous lectures that are available on YouTube. I posted a series where we toured his home library and discussed all his work, which you can also find on YouTube.

7. Or glosses, renderings, and equivalents.

8. The Jehovah's Witnesses' New World Translation is popular but is not a faithful translation of the original languages. It changes meanings at times, especially in the passages that affirm Christ's deity.

9. I identify *The Message* as a paraphrase, not a translation. *The Message* attempts to pick up the connotative value of the original, though it sometimes misses the mark. It is not intended to be a study Bible, but one that we can read paragraph by paragraph to get the feel of the original language.

The trick to understanding differences between all of these versions is to know their translation approach. Do you translate the main idea, the words, or both?

Rule of Thumb 2: Translations Are on a Spectrum

When I think about our misconceptions around Bible translations, this quote from *Finding Nemo* comes to mind: "Fish are friends, not food." Similarly, translations are tools, not tricks. (Say it in the shark's Australian accent—trust me, it's worth it!)

What does this mean? Well, our Bibles were originally written in different languages. As most translators know, there is no such thing as a perfect one-for-one translation between languages.

I spent a summer in Addis Ababa, Ethiopia, and there were times when we worked exclusively through translators to teach English to young children. I remember struggling through a grammar lesson one day, and when I said something about prepositions, all my students laughed at me! This was one of the few times when I was trying to be serious, and for the rest of the lesson I was insecure about what exactly had been mistranslated that turned out to be a joke.

Another day, my translator had an especially hard time translating my lesson, so he asked a peer to aid him. I was dumbfounded to see them both attempt to interpret what I was teaching using very different Amharic (a native language in Ethiopia) translations. I remember thinking, *I said one sentence—why are they speaking so long? Why is he saying something different from the other translator?* But this happened because language is dynamic!

From sentence structure to word order to imperfect equivalents, translation can get messy. Especially between ancient and modern languages. Idioms,[10] for example, often don't work in another language.[11] Therefore, when trying to translate complex ideas and concepts from ancient Greek (New Testament) or Hebrew (Old Testament),[12] it's essential to understand that there is no perfect translation. This is a common misconception for many Christians.

I want you to have assurance that what you are reading is the reliable Word of God, but I am not going to lie to you and tell you there's a perfect translation somewhere out there. Every translation of the Bible has come into our world with a different history of how and why it was compiled. Each translation has been influenced by unique theological and even political ideas. I highly recommend reading *Bible Translations for Everyone: A Guide to Finding a Bible That's Right for You* by Tim Wildsmith. It walks readers through some of the most popular translations and the histories behind them and gives helpful information about their various characteristics.

When translating between languages, there will always be different ideas about how to translate a concept and which words to use. A classic example involves the word *love*. I use

---

10. An idiom is a phrase or expression whose meaning isn't directly tied to the literal meanings of its words but is understood culturally or contextually (e.g., "kick the bucket" means "die").

11. For example, in Matthew 1:18 our English Bible translations say something along the lines of "She was found to be pregnant." But literally the Greek is "She was found to be having [it] in the belly."

12. This is, broadly speaking, a good rule of thumb, but other languages are used as well, such as Aramaic.

love to describe the way I feel about my husband—and the way I feel about pizza. Now, while I do love my homemade gluten-free pizza topped with dairy-free cheese and turkey pepperoni, I must admit I don't love it as much as I love my hunk of a husband. It's not fair to use the same word to describe both my feelings for my husband and my feelings for pizza. That is why many languages don't use the same word to denote different kinds of love, as English does.

In ancient Greek there were at least four words for love, depending on the situation or context. Words are nuanced! Language, history, culture, and so much more shape the use of even one simple word, especially in Hebrew.

The closest thing to a word-for-word translation is an interlinear Bible, which displays the original word next to the English word. You can find it printed and also free online. And yet this "translation" is not readable because sentence word order is so different in Greek and Hebrew. Even if you were to read it, you'd miss the meanings of the Bible's idioms, references, and allusions.

Here is an example of an interlinear Bible passage, the all-important Great Commission of Matthew 28:19–20: "Having gone therefore, disciple all the nations, baptizing them in the name of the Father, and of the Son, and of the Holy Spirit, teaching them to observe all things, whatever I commanded you. And behold, I with you am all the days until the completion of the age."[13]

As you can imagine, it is easy to get the wrong message from a passage when the words are out of normal English sentence order. There is a need for translations that take into

---

13. Interlinear Bible, under "Matthew 28:19," "Matthew 28:20," Bible Hub, accessed May 6, 2025, https://biblehub.com/interlinear/matthew/28-19.htm.

consideration the original intentions of Scripture's authors. That means we care about not only word-for-word translation but also thought-for-thought translation. We need the meaning, or sense, to be preserved. While we definitely want to be faithful to the original words, we don't want to do that at the expense of meaning. For example, I could tell you, "The preacher hit the nail on the head in his sermon." But if this is translated to someone of another culture who doesn't understand what "hitting the nail on the head" means, we lose the value of the literal word-for-word translation. This is the problem translators face at times: Translate the literal words or the meaning? Literal does not always mean faithful.[14] Most try to find a balance between the two, but some veer toward translating meaning more than others. This is why we want a good balance between the translator's approach to word-for-word *and* thought-for-thought translation. These two approaches serve as checks and balances that help us be as faithful to the text as possible.

Bible translation includes a spectrum of approaches. All of these attempt to balance accuracy,[15] literary quality,[16] and readability.[17] On one end are word-for-word translations, called

---

14. Daniel B. Wallace, in the preface to the NET Bible (first edition, 2005), explains, "Part of the problem is this: the more literal a translation is, the less readable it generally is; the more readable it is, the less faithful it is to the original meaning (at least in many cases). Some modern translations are quite readable but are not very faithful to the biblical author's meaning. A major goal of good translation is of course readability—but not at the expense of the intended meaning."

15. Accuracy means faithfulness to the original meaning and context. Both ends of the spectrum can neglect this. If we believe the Bible is true, we will want the meaning not to be changed but to be preserved through language.

16. Literary quality refers to how suitable it is for reading aloud, studying, memorizing, and so on.

17. Readability refers to how easy it is to read and understand the passage. The interlinear Bible, for example, is not very readable. The less readable, the more likely to be misunderstood. If we believe the Bible is true, we will want it to be properly understood.

formal equivalence, and on the other end are thought-for-thought translations, called *dynamic equivalence*. Figure 2.1 shows the ten most popular translations on this spectrum.

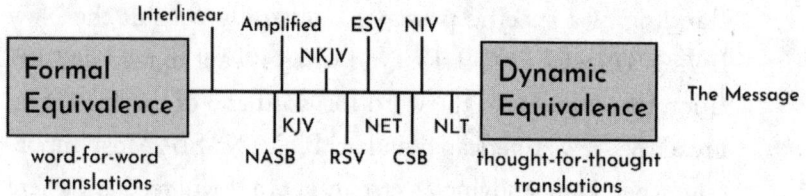

While I need to acknowledge that placement can vary based on personal opinion and preference, these placements are adapted from many different charts as well as my experience studying these translations.

Big picture: The translations closer to the formal-equivalence end of the spectrum are often harder to understand and therefore easier to misuse or misinterpret, while those closer to the dynamic-equivalence end veer farther from the exact words used because their purpose is to communicate clearly the thoughts and ideas conveyed in the original text. You will also notice that *The Message* Bible by Eugene Peterson is far past the dynamic-equivalence end of the spectrum. That's because it is a paraphrase of what the Bible says, rather than a true translation. But it can be a helpful resource for casual reading or when you need to see a passage with new eyes. My husband occasionally reads *The Message* to his youth group if they are struggling with the meaning of a passage or trying to figure out how it applies to their lives.

Now, if you are anything like me, you may be tempted to pick a translation from the left-hand side of the chart and ignore all the others. But this doesn't take into consideration the fact that *all* of these resources are for our use and benefit. I suggest using multiple translations. For my main Bible study, I use the English Standard Version (ESV). Yet I prefer the New International Version (NIV).[18] When I want a clearer understanding of a specific passage, I generally consult the New Living Translation (NLT). And when I want to read a translation that is closer to the word-for-word end of the spectrum, I read the New American Standard Bible (NASB). Most important, when I am studying a verse in-depth, I will read anywhere from five to ten different translations and compare all their differences[19] and similarities.

The different biblical translations are tools for our edification and enrichment. Remember my *Finding Nemo* reference? Translations are tools, not tricks! I would rather see someone who is struggling to open her Bible use the NLT than not read her Bible at all. I'll also reiterate that there is no one perfect translation. Too many well-meaning pastors and teachers have created a sense of fear and rage against some translations and put too much trust in others. You are a student of the Bible who wants to know God's Word and study it faithfully, so you can use the whole host of tools the Lord has equipped you with. Just as the church is built of Pentecostals, Presbyterians, and Baptists, so also it is equipped with many different Bible translations. So be encouraged—you can't mess this up! Your salvation

---

18. Your main Bible doesn't have to be your favorite translation. (This mentality assumes you're reading only one translation and avoiding the others.) But if Bible versions are tools, you'll be using different translations every day. Your favorite translation will change over time, but the tools won't. So use them all!

19. When the translations differ, especially if there are big differences, that tells me that the translators struggled to translate it—likely because it conveys a more complex idea that is not easily translatable. This is where I dig deeper into studying the Greek and Hebrew. But I am getting ahead of myself—we will get to that farther along in this book!

is not contingent on your reading the perfect translation perfectly. You were saved by the atonement Christ bought for you on the cross.

Rule of Thumb 3:
Don't Miss the Forest for the Trees

Translations are often treated like camps or tribes. Some people have made me feel as though I am a crazy liberal for reading the NLT, and others have treated me like some antiquated legalist for reading the KJV. But both of those responses negate rule of thumb 1 (reliability) and rule of thumb 2 (translations are on a spectrum). They negate the fact that the Bible itself is truth being translated through various methods *in order to preserve* truth. They also negate what the real focus should be when we talk about translations. Translations (even outside the world of biblical study) are tools for transmitting information. Let's not get so distracted about the translations themselves that we forget we're talking about the authoritative, infallible Word of God! The focus really should be this: Are we reading and believing the Word of God?

If we're really reading and believing the Word of God, we'll see that it's not about culture wars over Bible-translation philosophy but about the life-changing truth declared in the Bible. Friend, my aim in sharing these rules of thumb is to give ourselves permission to read Scripture and seek to delight in it.

You also need to know that you are worth it. You deserve to really know the Bible and understand those hard passages. You also don't have to be a Greek scholar or a pastor to understand

God's Word. The Bible is our anchor, our truth, our heritage, and our story.

Our Story

I have always been a scrapbooker. I started scrapbooking in fourth grade. What even was there to scrapbook back then? I was ten! But I loved capturing memories and feelings on a page with photos and stickers to retell the stories of my life that I didn't want to forget. Memory issues run in my family, and most of my grandparents have suffered from Alzheimer's or dementia. I've grown up knowing that it is likely, unless modern medicine prevents it, that I will live out the final years of my life unaware of my family and my identity, and I'll probably be just plain ol' cranky. If you're the kind nurse who one day brings me my morning medicine, I want to personally apologize in advance for what I say—there's no telling what will come out of this mouth! Just sing me some Shania Twain and I'll be happy.

I say all of this because I am keenly aware of the value of story. I don't want to forget my story, so I retell it through scrapbooking in order to remember it. Story tells us where we've been, where we are going, and who we are. Similarly, the Bible preaches to us that our belonging is not in this world, telling us the history of the people and kingdom of God and revealing his character along the way. The Bible also tells us what we can look forward to. All of this is what we will unpack in our next chapter, but we miss our identity as God's children, the history of our spiritual family, and the promises of what's coming if we don't read the story. So don't fall prey to the lies around translation. Just read the Bible.

Bible Nerd Notes

1. **RECAP.** Let's review some of the words we discussed in this chapter. *Inerrancy* describes the belief that the original Scriptures are without error, while *infallibility* describes the belief that the Bible's purpose, message, and promises are true. These are core aspects of my *hermeneutic*—how one reads and interprets the Bible. *Textual criticism* is the study of variants, or differences, in the preserved manuscripts of the Bible. The two ends of the Bible translation spectrum are *formal equivalence* (the word-for-word approach) and *dynamic equivalence* (the thought-for-thought approach).

2. **INVESTIGATE.** If you are curious about the world of Bible translators, I encourage you to check out the New English Translation (NET) Bible, Full Notes Edition, by Thomas Nelson. This Bible has tons of footnotes that take you into the minds of translators who discuss issues in biblical translation as well as explain what decisions they made and why.

3. **REFLECT.** Google "Interlinear translation of John 3:16." What do you notice about the word-for-word translation of this popular verse and how it is different from what you first read or memorized? How could the meaning be different, or changed, if left up to just the word-for-word translation?

4. **COMPARE.** Take a look at the following two translations of Romans 5:8. They each use a different verb to translate συνίστησιν *(synistēsin)* (what God did with his love).

   ○ NIV: "But God <u>demonstrates</u> his own love for us in this: While we were still sinners, Christ died for us."

   ○ CSB: "But God <u>proves</u> his own love for us in that while we were still sinners, Christ died for us."

Does God *demonstrate* his love or *prove* it? Both the NIV and the CSB translate from the same Greek text.[20] The Greek συνίστησιν *(synistēsin)*, when translated, is defined in *Strong's Concordance* as "conveying the idea of bringing together or establishing something. In the New Testament, it is often used in the context of commending or demonstrating, particularly in relation to character or actions. It can also imply the act of proving or showing something to be true or valid."[21]

As you can see, the NIV uses the word *demonstrates* as a faithful translation of the Greek, but the CSB, though not very far from it on our translations spectrum, uses the word *proves*. Both are fair translations, which we see in the definition. The CSB might make better sense to some readers than the NIV, which aims to use a closer synonym. Both translations, however, serve us in building a faithful theology of Christ's work and love.

---

20. That is, the critical text from the United Bible Societies and Nestle-Aland.

21. *Strong's Exhaustive Concordance,* "4921. sunistémi and sunistanó," https://biblehub.com/greek/4921.htm. *Strong's* is the most popular resource for biblical studies on the specific words used throughout the Bible.

CHAPTER 3

Your New Reading Glasses

My son Sutton got glasses at age three, and it made his cute score (if there was one) explode beyond what I'd ever thought was possible. It also opened my eyes to how much he couldn't see before. No wonder he had a hard time going up and down stairs! No wonder he would always stand close to the TV instead of snuggling with Momma and Daddy! His poor brain couldn't compute the blurry images he was seeing from a distance. How much had he missed out on? I had all sorts of mom guilt that my sweet Sutton had needed glasses and I'd had no idea—I just thought it was his unique personality to stand so close to the TV!

His optometrist explained to me that one of Sutton's eyes was not really working, and therefore the other eye was doing all the work. The weaker eye would essentially "turn off" if it wasn't able to pull its own weight. My son would go half blind-ish without his glasses. Now, it is highly likely I just botched that explanation, but we are going to roll with it because it makes an excellent illustration for this chapter's opening.

Many Christians today are walking around with a similar blindness. We (often subconsciously) think the Bible is too hard to understand or too boring to read. We sometimes automatically assume we're supposed to dislike the Old Testament and struggle through the details of Revelation. It's like we're squinting at the Bible trying to find what we think we're supposed to find instead of seeing clearly what is presented there. If we're not careful, we may go half blind to the true meaning. Instead of squinting and leaning in too close, asking, "Why don't I understand this?" or "What does this mean for me?" let's step back, put on our new glasses, and look at the Bible with a newfound 20/20 vision.

The Bible Made Simple

The story of the Bible can be summarized in one phrase: the story of God redeeming his people for his glory.[1] When you look at the Bible as one big narrative,[2] made up of smaller stories, you'll see it is all about God saving his people. In a perfect three-act story structure,[3] the subject is God, the problem is our

---

1. I am not sure where I got this phrase, but it is definitely from someone else, not me.

2. Though I use words such as *narrative* and *story*, that doesn't mean I think the Bible isn't true or inerrant. Rather, these terms highlight the literary nature of the Bible.

3. Popularized by the Greek philosopher Aristotle, this story structure has a beginning, middle action and tension, and an ending resolution. There have been numerous modern additions to this story structure, but the same basic concept remains true: Humans are hardwired to respond to a story beginning with a character facing a problem and ending with their conquering it. The Bible, when evaluated on a macro scale, is also written/compiled using this same structure.

sin that has corrupted our relationship with a holy God, and the story arc is of God rescuing and ransoming us back to himself.

Did you catch that? The Bible isn't primarily about us. We aren't the main characters. It's the story of *God* redeeming *his* people for *his* glory. Is it *for* us? Definitely. But it's not primarily *about* us. We are not the main characters of the story, so why do we open God's Word looking for ourselves?

Maybe you can't decide whether you should take a new job or not. So you open the Bible and read Jeremiah 29:11: "'For I know the plans I have for you,' declares the LORD, 'plans to prosper you and not to harm you, plans to give you hope and a future.'" But reading that verse only frustrates you because God isn't spelling out his plans for you more clearly. Or you're on the fence about dating a guy you recently met, so you turn to 1 Corinthians 16:14: "Do everything in love." But that only makes you wonder whether you're supposed to have a friendship or a romantic relationship with the guy.

Some of us may be wondering, "Why didn't God spend more time laying out who I'm supposed to date, what major I should choose in college, and where I should live?" But this is because we have been fed the lie (through culture) that everything we do, including reading the Bible, should be about us. But if I open the Bible and immediately look for myself in it, is that really worship? If I go to the Bible looking for answers only during times of personal crisis, is that showing faith-filled dependence on God, or is it treating him like he's a magic genie? Going to the Bible only looking for solutions to our problems is taking the Bible that displays the story of God redeeming his people for his glory and manipulating it to be our own story. It's for you, but it's not about you; it's about him! And, ironically enough, if we read those passages in context and look at what the Bible actually says, it will end up affecting who we date, what major we choose, and where we should live. But it will also do so much more. Reading the Bible and seeing how it really is all about God makes our interpretation and application so much more powerful.

What Is Your Hermeneutic?

All of this discussion about the story of the Bible and what we are looking for in God's Word is part of our hermeneutic. As a reminder, our hermeneutic is how we understand and approach the text to interpret it. If you believe that Revelation only prophesies future events, you will treat it differently than those who believe a fair bit of the book covers what happened in AD 70. Or if you believe the Bible is not true, you will read it in a different way than someone who assumes that the Bible is God's inerrant Word. How you view the Bible affects how you read it, and this in turn affects how you interpret what you read. Another word for interpretation is *exegesis*. When a pastor reads the Bible and says, "This means . . ." the pastor is doing exegesis.[4] When we are at home reading the Bible and seeking to understand how it applies to our own lives, we are doing exegesis. Everyone does exegesis. Both exegesis and hermeneutics are done by everyone, most of the time subconsciously. But we are stronger students in our hermeneutics and exegesis when we become aware of our

---

4. Note that exegesis is different from application. *Exegesis* is the explanation or understanding of the message, while *application* is the working out of the message in one's life. There should be one meaning behind the words (excluding prophecies and literary tools such as puns), but there can be many applications.

hermeneutic and subsequent exegesis based on our presuppositions around the Bible. Do we believe it's true? Do we believe it's about us? Or, rather, for us? These are questions we must evaluate to have a faithful hermeneutic.

As you can see, our exegesis is shaped by our beliefs. If I believe the Bible is true (part of my hermeneutic), my exegesis will be far different from the exegesis of my atheist friends, though we may read the same Bible verses. Additionally, a theological progressive and a theological conservative will both have different approaches to many texts. Egalitarians[5] and traditional complementarians[6] will treat texts differently. That is because we aren't robots merely taking in information. We all have biases, traumas, beliefs, and worldviews that inform our reading of the Bible, whether we realize it or not.

Often at this point I will hear comments like "Well, that is why my pastor preaches unbiased!" Friend, do not be deceived. No one reads the Bible without their own preconceived ideas. Even pastors! If they act like they are unbiased, they are more dangerous and less trustworthy than those who are open about their biases. That is why I opened this book by saying I believe in inerrancy and infallibility.[7] Can you read this book if you don't believe the same? Absolutely! Can you be a believer? Sure!

---

5. Those who believe women have the same leadership roles in the home and church as men.

6. Those who believe the inherent created differences in men and women are also mirrored in marriage, home, and church leadership roles.

7. Remember, these are the beliefs that the Bible is reliable. The Bible isn't lying or deceptive. The truth of the Word is something I can stake my soul on. While scribes have misspelled words, humans have mindlessly thrown away parchments, and the Bible has been translated from the original languages, the original document is inerrant and the message is infallible. As John Frame says in his chapter "The Inerrancy of Scripture" in *The Doctrine of the Word of God* (Phillipsburg, NJ: P&R, 2010), "When we say that the Bible is inerrant, we mean that the Bible makes good on its claims" (174).

But I must acknowledge the obvious bias I have—that I believe the Bible to be infallible.

The final word I want you to know is *eisegesis*. Eisegesis is like exegesis; however, it is "me-centered." It means we're reading *into* the text rather than out of it. We're studying the text looking for ourselves, our understandings, or our modern culture.[8] Put simply, eisegesis is when we insert our own ideas, biases, or agendas into the text. (Eisegesis isn't a good thing!)

Here's an example of eisegesis: the critics of the church who say that Jesus was showing homosexual love whenever he kissed the disciples. Some of them say the same thing about David and Jonathan. But that understanding of a kiss—as sexual—is a twenty-first-century Western worldview. We need to be careful not to read our modern-day understandings of the world into the way we read the Bible, because we aren't reading a modern text! We are reading an ancient book that had ancient expectations for greetings (such as a kiss). We need to figure out what the first-century or ancient Near Eastern people were understanding from the passage, not automatically assume we know everything.

Now, there is a big exception to this: The prophecies of Jesus at times were not understood to always be prophecies of the Messiah. There were times when the prophets probably thought they were pronouncing metaphors of hope, and then Jesus came and fulfilled them literally.[9] There are other times when King

---

8. This can look like the previously discussed misuse of Philippians 4:13 or even be Origen's multiple meanings and allusions he'd read into passages. There are tons of ways we can do eisegesis, but most commonly it comes from neglecting context like genre, culture, and the intended message of the author.

9. This is often referred to as *sensus plenior*—the fuller meaning of the text, not found in the literal words. We, however, can see the fuller meaning of the Old Testament only by the revelation of the New Testament. We cannot assume all texts have hidden meanings we can construct (or "reveal") unless they are otherwise made clear by the intertextuality of the Bible itself.

David was writing his prayers and praise, and then Jesus came and quoted them.[10] But now we read those texts and can understand the original historical settings as well as the fulfillments of Jesus in them.

For the most part, however, if we want to be faithful to the Bible, we need to be wary about falsely assuming that we always know the intentions of the text. There are thousands of years of history and culture between us today and the people of the Bible, and we shouldn't always assume we know what they meant. We need to do our own due diligence to make sure our interpretation (and subsequent application) is as faithful as possible to the intention of the passage, or else we are just making it say what we think it should say.

That sentence may have sounded sassy to you. I'm not going to apologize, but I will back it up with an explanation for my sass: We are *freed* to find so much more richness in Scripture when we look at the truths in Scripture outside of us. The Bible is so much bigger than us. We cheat ourselves when we aim for only an elementary understanding of the biblical truths. Some people tell me they don't use resources in Bible study because the Holy Spirit is the only thing believers need to understand the Word, often misusing 1 John 2:27. While I believe in the perspicuity of Scripture (this is a term that means Scripture is clear enough for anyone to understand salvation), I am not going to act as if the Holy Spirit downloads information on the exile and imports it into my brain when I read Isaiah 40. If we believe the Bible is true, we will engage joyfully in the studious "work" of making sure we are faithful to it.

---

10. See Psalm 22:1 and 110:1.

Let me give you an example. Ruth is a book of the Bible that is beloved among many women's ministries. Many women read it to learn how they can have the loyalty of Ruth. They admire her boldness and God's faithful provision through Boaz. They ask themselves whether they are like Ruth; who might their Boaz be; and where they might be called to cling to a Naomi. This is a shallow understanding of the text, however. Adele Berlin argues that Ruth isn't even the main character of this book. She says the real main character is Naomi![11]

You see, when you read this book looking only for your application, you miss the message. When you look past an elementary understanding, you realize the story isn't about Ruth being a "good girl" who is loyal enough to be rewarded with Boaz. Rather, it is about a woman, Naomi, whose husband led her and her family out of the holy land of Bethlehem. Naomi's husband didn't trust God to provide in a famine, so he brought his family from Bethlehem (which, ironically, means "house of bread") to the Canaanite plains of Moab. There, he and his sons died.[12] In this ancient Near Eastern culture, a woman would be taken care of by her sons when she lost her husband. But Naomi also lost her sons, so there was no one to provide for her. She also had two dead-weight daughters-in-law now following her around.

Because of all this loss, Naomi heads back to God's land to try to survive the famine. She tells her daughters-in-law not to come with her because no good Hebrew man would marry a

---

11. Adele Berlin, "Ruth—Big Theme, Little Book," *Bible Review* 12, no. 4 (August 1996): 20–29.

12. Did you catch the irony of leaving the "house of bread" in a famine? Furthermore, Bethlehem is the birthplace of Jesus, the one who would later proclaim himself to be the Bread of Life (John 6:35)!

Moabite (Canaanite) woman. Ruth stays with Naomi despite her persistent urging for her to go back to her pagan land and gods. Naomi and Ruth go back to Bethlehem, and the Lord provides bread and grain through his glorious law,[13] as well as connects Naomi and Ruth with a kinsman-redeemer (family redeemer). At the beginning of the book of Ruth, Naomi is empty and hopeless (she even declares this in Ruth 1:21), and at the end of the book, not only has she been provided for, but she now has a lineage—a "son" and a grandson (Ruth 4:17).

Do you see how the story is far deeper than just a call to "be loyal"? Do you also see how this is the story of God redeeming his people for his glory, not just a story about Ruth?

More important, the book of Ruth was written to point to the Davidic kingly line, highlighting how King David came from this bloodline. Naomi is David's great-great-grandmother. We can read it today knowing the Messiah came from the line of David and is the greater fulfillment of the provision displayed throughout this book. Just as God did not leave Naomi empty (Ruth 1:21) but filled her up with blessings and provisions beyond what she could have ever hoped (4:17), God, too, has met us in our emptiness and depravity with a Redeemer who came from this very bloodline!

We cheapen the book of Ruth when we read it as if it were written only to encourage women to be faithful daughters and wives. While that's a small anecdote of application, it doesn't scratch the surface of the depths of the riches found in those pages of the Bible. The original audience would have understood all of this through the closing genealogy, which ends the book

---

13. Deuteronomy 24:19 calls the harvesters to leave some grain behind for the foreigners, orphans, and widows to glean.

as the "happily ever after" pointing to David. We cheapen the richness of the promises of God's provision when we make it about just Ruth's or our loyalty.

The real comfort of the book of Ruth is that God sees us in our destitute emptiness, the place where there seems to be no hope, and he is working out his plans for the hope of the world (Jesus). God works through details we don't even realize or see in the moment. God is always providing redemption.

See how this reframes our focus from ourselves and our own ability to be good little Ruths and sets it instead on God's good love and provision? See also how much of a richer, more encouraging Bible study this becomes?

Deeper Study Is God-Study

This depth in study comes from seeing what Scripture is saying about God. Through seeing God's actions in dealing with unfaithful Naomi or his mercy dealing with Ruth, we see his great wisdom and love—and that informs the decisions we make and reshapes the struggles we face. But it all starts with seeing who God is in Scripture and then living changed by that. Please hear that my heart is not against us living out our faith. Rather, my heart is for us not to cheapen Scripture into just a moral code of conduct. Scripture is about the one who transforms us. Scripture declares truths about him that change the way we live, but that change starts with our understanding him and how he works in, through, and despite us.

If God called both Ruth and Abraham out of their homelands to follow him at all costs, then maybe where I live and work isn't that big of a deal.[14] Maybe I need to be ready to leave it behind at any time to follow him because he is a God that works in and through nothingness. If Jacob worked for fourteen years before he could marry Rachel, maybe it's not as much about getting the wedding and happily ever after as it is about being faithful and patient wherever God has placed us, because God is always at work. If God was able to use a large fish to swallow unfaithful Jonah and put him back on the path to Nineveh, then maybe it's not about our taking the right steps forward but rather about our taking whatever steps we take in faith, because he will pivot us if needed.[15] So while you read and ask yourself "What does this mean for my life?" see how the application of the Bible in our lives should always be based on the truths displayed about God. It isn't that the Bible doesn't help us with our decisions, but we minimize God's Word when we open it up *only* to find solutions to our problems.

The Bible is so much more than just a map to follow or a clue book in which God gives us hints about what to do. When you read the Bible, you can see through story after story that God is not dependent on our hearing his hints and doing the perfect thing; rather, he works in, through, and despite us. Friend, the Bible is not just an old, dead, boring book we "ought" to read. It is alive and active,[16] God-breathed,[17] and it never passes away.[18]

---

14. Of course it is important, but it isn't the be-all and end-all.

15. This does not let us off the hook from faithful obedience when God has given us a clear call; Jonah was acting in disobedience. But if God can pivot Jonah in his disobedience, how much more can God redirect us when we are walking in faith and obedience!

16. Hebrews 4:12.

17. 2 Timothy 3:16.

18. Matthew 24:35.

Praise the Lord that his Word is not an old, dead, boring book! Praise the Lord that it is not just about us! Yes, the Bible is a book that answers all our major questions about life, but it is also a crucial book of truth for all people. I pray that this framework of the Bible (as the story of God redeeming his people for his glory) will set you free from the shackles of me-centric reading. This is what I like to refer to as a *biblical worldview*. This means that the Bible gives us a way to view the world and understand our roles in it. But this framework of the Bible is crucial to build from as we move on to talking about the story outline of the Bible.

The story of the Bible has four parts: It starts with Creation, moves on to the Fall, follows with Redemption, and closes with Consummation.[19] Every part of the Bible can be placed in one of these categories, which ends up affecting how we view the Bible and the world. Let's discover those in the next chapter. In the meantime, I invite you to join me in praising God that the Bible is so much more than just a rule book. It is the story of God redeeming his people for his glory, and if you've trusted in Jesus Christ and his work on the cross for salvation, *you* are his people. The Bible is the story revealing how God redeems, just like he has redeemed you. Therefore, every page of the Bible deserves a worshipful response, as we praise him that he didn't leave us empty (think of Naomi in Ruth 1:21) but has ransomed us.

---

19. This is often a word we use exclusively to refer to a romantic relationship and sexual intercourse. In the context of a contract, however, it means that all the requirements of the contract have been completed. Theologically speaking, this is the idea we have in mind. Consummation is when the promises have been kept, everything is complete, and we have the close, intimate relationship with the Lord that is better than any sexual, romantic relationship could bring.

Bible Nerd Notes
〰〰〰〰〰〰

1. **RECAP.** The Bible as a whole can be summarized as the story of God redeeming his people for his glory. Consider writing this on the inside cover of your Bible or on a sticky note to place where you'll be reminded often of this truth. This is such a powerful truth because every book of the Bible plays a part in revealing this story of God redeeming his people. Next time you're lost in your Bible reading and don't know what you're supposed to get from it, ask yourself, "How does this passage show a part of the story of God redeeming his people for his glory?" Sometimes a passage shows a small bit of redemption (think of the books of Ezra and Nehemiah); other times a passage shows us the need for redemption (Genesis 3) or God's glory (Job 38).

2. **REFLECT.** In this chapter I attempted to convince you that reading the Bible as the story of God redeeming his people for his glory transforms our hermeneutic (and following exegesis) to be less me-centric—and that this is a much richer reading of the Bible. Consider Jonah: Famous for running away from God, Jonah is a prophet called to prophesy to a people he hates. But instead of obeying God, he sails in the opposite direction. When a storm comes, he immediately interprets it as God's judgment on him, but instead of repenting, Jonah becomes so depressed that he tells the sailors, "Throw me overboard!" because he'd rather die than head to Nineveh. A large fish swallows him, he's inside the fish for a couple of days, and then he repents and goes to Nineveh after the fish spits him out. (Yes, he was brought so low he was fish vomit!)

While many simplify the book of Jonah down to the general lesson of "Don't disobey God," there is so much more going on in the text. In fact, Jonah never really seems to learn his lesson because when he does prophesy to the Ninevites, they miraculously repent—and he throws a fit! You see, the book isn't to be read as some kind of "be like repentant Jonah and go to your Nineveh!" lesson. At the end of the book, Jonah is still just as depressed and belligerent as he was at the beginning, and we are left wondering, "Did he ever learn?"

Actually, the book of Jonah is all about God. It begins with the word of the Lord calling Jonah (1:1) and ends with God's speech (4:9–11). Even when Jonah runs away, it's always in reference to God's presence (see 1:3). Additionally, the book continually shows us God's actions "appointing" a storm, a fish, and a plant (see 1:4, 17; 2:10; 4:6–8). Even when Jonah tries to throw a fit and verbally attack God, he says, "I knew you were gracious and merciful, slow to anger, and abounding in steadfast love!" (see 4:2). Is that really supposed to be some sort of insult, Jonah?

The book of Jonah is so much richer than just "Don't run away from God." Scan through the book now and see what else you notice in the text that puts the focus on God, not us. Bonus points if you read the entire book and take notes on some of the things I mentioned. It's so short and very worth it.

3. **COMPARE.** After looking at Jonah a little deeper, we see it is the story of how God worked in, through, and despite Jonah. But reading Jonah knowing that it's about God and not us does not mean it doesn't change us or transform our hearts. Notice the similarities between Jonah and Christ: Both were from Galilee (2 Kings 14:25; Matt. 21:11); both preached to Jews *and* gentiles (Jonah 1:2; Eph. 2:17); both slept in boats during a storm

(Jonah 1:5; Matt. 8:23–27); both had lots cast over them (Jonah 1:7; Matt. 27:35); both spent three days in a lowly place—Jonah in the belly of a fish and Jesus in a tomb (Jonah 1:17; Matt. 12:40); and both were called to prophesy truth. One did it begrudgingly, suicidal at the thought of Ninevite repentance and God's mercy (Jonah 4:3), while the other did so willingly. Jesus was perfectly obedient to the will of the Father (John 6:38), laying down his life for our ransom (1 John 3:16).

The book of Jonah shows us God's nature of love and kindness despite Jonah's seemingly rightful hatred, and it also shows us how Jesus is the greater, perfect prophet. He genuinely desires the salvation of the undeserving, which is us. We are the undeserving. We are the unfit Ninevites whom Jesus went to great lengths to reach. This is the difference that reading the Bible in this framework—a story about God, for us—makes. Now, praise God for this good news. He loves us that deeply.

CHAPTER 4

The Storyline of the Bible

After being married for almost a decade, my husband and I have grown this ability to read each other's minds with just a simple look. If he gives me a certain look when he's having a stern talk with one of our sons, I know it's time to step in and take over the parenting. If I roll my head in a circle around my shoulders, he knows I'm exhausted and need some grace . . . and a shoulder rub. These are things we've learned through the thick and thin of life—including having kids, doing church ministry, and seeing each other's full depravity. We've learned how to communicate with each other in ways we'd never imagined previously. And if this is only ten years in, I can't imagine what it'll be like in thirty!

Similarly, the storyline of the Bible—Creation, Fall, Redemption, and Consummation—is the secret code to understanding the communication of the Bible. Think of these as chapters in the story of God redeeming his people for his glory.

These four chapters are all critical to understanding where the Bible has been and where it's going.

Similar to how my relationship with my husband—after ten years together, two kids, and seven moves—is so much deeper now than it was when we were dating, so also is the story of the Bible in Revelation 22 compared to Genesis 1. The Bible isn't stagnant, but the Prophets build off the Pentateuch and its theology, which is built upon by the Gospel writers and also in the letters. The story builds. If you miss one point, you won't understand what's going on or why there seems to be secret weird communication or words (just like between my husband and me). For example, a large chunk of Revelation alludes to other parts of the Bible. Just like a relationship looks different through different seasons of knowing the other person, so also has humankind's relationship with God changed and evolved.

Creation, Fall, Redemption, and Consummation (CFRC) defines four eras or chapters of the Bible's story, and they are crucial for us to understand so that we don't miss the intimate communication. It's part of the intimacy of the story of a loving God redeeming his people for his glory. Understanding the distinctives of each chapter of the story will help us understand God's good plan more fully.

Let's start with Creation. Genesis chapters 1 and 2 show us that God created all things in an orderly fashion, then rested. So many of us open up to these chapters of Genesis to defend our views on creation and the age of the earth, but we fail to see that there's so much more going on here. These chapters tell us that God was before all things, created all things (including the things we don't know, the things we fear, and the things that give us anxiety), and created us for that perfect garden world.

This part of the Bible not only comforts us that God in his ultimate wisdom, power, and truth rules over his creation but also reassures us that the tension we feel from day to day is because we weren't made for this. The longing inside our bones is for heaven. The hole we sense in the pit of our souls is there because we long for that union and peace with God in the garden.

The Story Starts with Creation

While I was writing this chapter, I was sitting at my desk in the early-morning sunlight, sipping my coffee. My four-year-old son had woken up early to join me. Maybe he was excited for a summer day filled with swimming and frog hunting, but all I knew was that he was up early writing his own book as he sat next to me. With his Crayola markers he drew all sorts of creatures and excitedly showed them off. Then he got an idea from a fish he'd drawn that looked awfully snuggly.

"I want a fish friend, Mom!" Sutton cried. "Can we go to PetSmart and get a fish?" Still trying to finish typing my sentence, I responded, "No, we have lots of pets already!" But we're still working on the issue of nagging in our family, so a couple of minutes and a few more requests for a fish passed before I realized just how serious he was about this pet. Sutton wanted to fill his bug catcher with water and carry his fish with him everywhere. He had it all planned out and just knew, as sure as everything, at 7:15 in the morning, that a fish would solve all his problems.

I am by no means all-wise and by no means the creator and sustainer of the earth, yet even I knew that this fish would soon end up dead and flushed down the toilet or, if it lasted longer than that, be a new burden for my husband and me to try to remember to feed. I held my breath—as I also tried to hold my attitude in check—and reminded my son that we had so many other pets. Two dogs, three kittens, ten goats, and nineteen chickens ought to have been enough! But no. Sutton continued to insist on the pet fish.

His eyes filled with tears as he realized I wasn't about to drop everything and take him to PetSmart immediately. I put my hands underneath his tiny arms and pulled him up onto my lap. And after a few minutes of discussion, we decided to make a pretend fish out of Legos before going to the pet store.

Thankfully, he eventually forgot about the fish and moved on to a new adventure, but it gave me a good picture of what Genesis chapters 1 and 2 do for us believers. We walk through this life tired, weary, overwhelmed, and desperate for aid. We grip so tightly to our ideas of what we think will solve our problems and pray earnestly for God to give us our desires. But often these things we're praying for are like Sutton's fish. We have this idea of what we need or want, without the full knowledge of what taking care of a real-life pet would entail. We demand a new fish from PetSmart, thinking it will solve all our problems, and we petition the throne as if everything depends on it (because in our minds it does). But God, in his infinite wisdom, having made the entire universe, knows the fish isn't really what we need. He longs for us to rest in his wisdom and guidance and rely on him more fully. But it does take faith to believe that what God has for us is better than what we think we need. It takes trust that the one who made us and our circumstances will sometimes say no in love—and that this is the best thing for us.

These are some of the truths that Genesis chapters 1 and 2

preach to us. Though we are created and finite, our God is Creator and infinite. Though we don't see all the whys or hows, he knows it all and sustains it all. And this is good news. It is good news that we aren't here by chance. That there's a bigger story than our own. It's good news that it doesn't all depend on us. We can lay our heads on our pillows at night knowing there's a bigger picture, a story of redemption that God is working out, and it is a much better story than we could ever write.

Creation also gives us a picture of what God is working from and toward. The writers of Scripture often look back at Creation and long for that garden-like intimacy with God. Israel longed for it in Egyptian slavery, in the wilderness wanderings, in temple building, in the exile, and so on. The Bible moves from Creation to Consummation (heaven) because of the Fall. We're always longing to go back to Creation, to the time when Adam and Eve dwelt in the garden with the security and closeness of God's presence. The good news is that we get even better garden-like closeness looking forward, not backward. But, either way, we long for it. This is because of the curse of the Fall. So let's address the Fall.

The Ruin of Creation: The Fall

The next part of the Bible's story of God redeeming his people for his glory is the Fall. Most people know this one, whether they are churched or not. It's the story of one of the most undeniable realities of the human experience: sin. In our world we know sin all too well. Watch the news for less than a minute and you'll likely grow overwhelmed with all the accounts of sin and brokenness in our world. From robberies to shootings to wars, most—if not all—of us can profess that there is brokenness all around us.

In a panel discussion for Ligonier Ministries, R. C. Sproul once succinctly answered the question of how to explain sin to someone who rejects the idea: "Steal his wallet."[1] Now, I am not advising you to do the same. Stealing is obviously perpetuating the problem! But hopefully you get his point. We know sin best by seeing it where it hurts. Whether it is in our wallets, our pride, or our personal relationships, I'm sure we have all known the pain of sin in our lives.

For this part of the Bible story, which we call the Fall, we know from Genesis 3 that Adam and Eve ate the fruit of the forbidden tree in the garden and then "everything turned bad," as my son Winchester once put it. The Fall caused death and sickness, and all of creation continues to live under its consequences.[2] But, most tragically, the Fall hit us where it hurts most—in our relationship with God. We could no longer have a garden-like relationship with God because now we had a sinful nature and God cannot commune with brokenness. So Adam and Eve were sent out of the garden, and while they still had the same job as before the Fall (to steward and garden God's creation),[3] they now were doing it under the consequences of their actions.[4]

---

1. "How Do I Explain Sin to an Unbeliever?" Ligonier Ministries, March 26, 2014, https://www.youtube.com/watch?v=wqLst6RcBXA.

2. Romans 8:22.

3. This even informs how we understand work today. We were created to steward, build, and develop. That's why the Bible moves from garden to city. We are happiest when we do the stewarding we were created to do. That's why nothing left unkept keeps. That's why you get heavenly joy when you're creating. That's why the person without a sense of calling and direction is sometimes suicidal. God created us to have purpose and to work. Our lives are not meaningless or futile.

4. Notice how the curses of the Fall all pertain to the stewarding Adam and Eve were created to do (Gen. 1:28–30; 3:16–19).

For our hermeneutic, the era of the Fall spans all the way from Adam and Eve to the cross. Along the way, God made a covenant with his people to redeem them from the curse of the Fall. He began setting them apart and working through them, but they were still under the curse. Throughout the Old Testament we can see God working through the forefathers of the faith and revealing much about his love and nature to them. We see him make (and keep) promises to Abraham, Isaac, Jacob, Joseph, Moses, David, and so many others. Time and time again, God revealed himself to be a "compassionate and gracious God, slow to anger, abounding in love and faithfulness."[5] We see normal, even undeserving, men and women getting called and used by God despite the fact that they were a pagan moon worshiper (Abraham), a lowly Moabite outsider (Ruth), a lustful murderer (David), or a lying trickster (Jacob). Just look at the call of Abraham in Genesis 12 (fig. 4.1).

Genesis 12:1–4

Moon worshiping sinner!

"Leave behind your old identity".

[1] The LORD had said to Abram, "Go from your country, your people and your father's household to the land I will show you. [2] "I will make you into a great nation, and I will bless you;

Called and blessed to bless others

I will make your name great, and you will be a blessing. [3] I will bless those who bless you, and whoever curses you I will curse; and all peoples on earth will be blessed through you."

P.S. The blessing is Jesus.

[4] So Abram went, as the LORD had told him; and Lot went with him. Abram was seventy-five years old when he set out from Harran.

It's never too late for God to work in and through you.

5. Exodus 34:6–7. Notice how the rest of the Bible alludes to this repeatedly. These are key words and phrases that are used about God throughout the Bible.

Despite the fact that none of God's people seemed to deserve it, God kept his promises and delivered his people from slavery, danger, famine, and destruction over and over again. Through prophets, priests, and kings, God set up leaders and truth speakers.[6] Even through terrible times, such as the exile of Israel into Babylon, God was still faithful and kind to his people, refining them, calling them back to himself, and working his great plan of redemption.[7]

The era of the Fall might seem like a big block of time in history when God was doing "stuff" that doesn't really matter to us today. But book after book, chapter after chapter, line after line show us the thread of redemption. Throughout his Word, God is constantly redeeming his people for his glory. Take any book of the Bible, or any character in the Old Testament, and every inch of the story will play a role in pointing us toward Jesus. Through prophets, priests, kings, sinners, rebels, and penitents, we see God redeeming his people for his glory. It is all pointing to our need for a Savior, and that Savior is Jesus.

Many people like to break up this large block of time, and the Bible as a whole, into dispensations, or different eras, but I am of the party[8] that sees it all as one big plan of redemption, which was always one big promise of redemption through Jesus. We call this the covenant of redemption. Covenants are

---

6. Prophets (this includes judges), priests, and kings were called to speak truth and call God's people back to the law, obedience, and worship.

7. *Redemption* is a fancy word that means God bought us back (or ransomed us) to himself. The New Testament Greek word used for redemption is ἀπολύτρωσις *(apolutrósis)*, meaning release effected by payment of ransom, or a deliverance. Essentially, there was a price we couldn't pay, which Christ met with his own blood shed on the cross.

8. This "party" is referred to as *covenant theologians*. It is a way of viewing the Bible through the undeniable use of covenants God has made with his people, dependent on himself.

promises between two parties. We see God, time after time, make a covenant with his people. In the book of Deuteronomy, God uses the ancient Near Eastern suzerain treaty to set up his promises, or covenant, with his people.[9] And unlike the rest of the world with their treaties and promises, God makes and keeps promises with his people *by himself.*

What do I mean? Well, Adam and Eve eat the fruit, and then God kills an animal to cover their nakedness and promises redemption in the story chronicled in Genesis 3:15. After Noah receives God's promise to never again flood the earth, he then proceeds to get drunk and sin! But God made and kept his promise, not because Noah was sinless, but because God is just that good. He promises to make Abraham a great nation, and in Genesis 15 swears it by himself, while Abraham is asleep. Abraham brings nothing to the table. He is a moon worshiper[10] who is full of doubts and lies, but God still uses him despite himself. And look at Isaac and Jacob. God continues to reaffirm his promises to them as well—even though they are broken, undeserving sinners,[11] just the same as Abraham. God keeps his promises to his people despite themselves.

Next, Moses receives the law—a standard no one can perfectly follow but that nonetheless points to the only one who has followed it: Jesus. The law is rooted in the grace of God who saves us in his love and redemption and provides rules to live

---

9. This identification first came to prominence during the mid-1950s in the writings of American scholar George E. Mendenhall.

10. Abram came from Ur of the Chaldees, which is known as the center of worship of the false moon-god Nanna. Abram later turns to follow and worship the Lord, but his background is why it is so significant that he was called to leave his family and home (Gen. 12:1). The land where one's people group belonged was tied to the gods in the ancient Near Eastern culture.

11. See Genesis 26 and 27 for an example. These people are messed-up, selfish liars!

by as guideposts for the redeemed. Moses knows all too well his own unworthiness—and that of the people—yet God keeps his promises to his people despite their shortcomings and because of *God's* faithfulness. The covenant promises move on to David, a liar, cheater, and murderer.[12] Although he's a talented musician, this man is far from perfect, yet we see the kingdom aspect highlighted through him. God uses the imperfect David to point to the prophesied perfect King of an eternal throne: the Messiah.

Throughout the Old Testament we see sinners being sinners and God being God. His love never changes. His plan never does either. Through all of these forerunners[13] of the faith and many more, we see that God's heart has always been for redemption—ransoming sinners back to himself, despite themselves. With this in sight, we can see there is a beautiful created order, but there is always the problem of sin, and we all instinctively seek a resolution or happy ending to the brokenness.

The Cost of the Fall Met in Redemption

This leads us to the next part of the story, which is Redemption. Remember: *Redemption* is a word that means God bought us back—or ransomed us—to himself. What was the price he paid for us, and where was the exchange done? The cross. The cross is an important part of this story because this is where our redemption was bought by Christ when he laid down his life as the payment for our sins. It is the solution to the Fall and the reality we live in today. And the cross isn't the end of the story.

---

12. See 2 Samuel 11.
13. See Hebrews 11:1–12:1.

Redemption starts with the incarnation—God humbling himself in the form of a baby. Jesus wasn't born to an earthly throne (though earthly thrones come nowhere close to a heavenly throne); he was born in one of the humblest towns in one of the most challenging but important eras of history. God decided before all time that he would redeem his people for his glory through the incarnation. So Jesus came, lived, ministered, died a sinner's death, and broke the grave open. Then he ascended into heaven, promising that his Holy Spirit would come and bring the Eden-like intimacy between God and man back to his people, getting even closer than God and Adam could: with the Holy Spirit living inside us.[14]

Romans 5 talks about how sin came into the world through one man, Adam, and now eternal life can come to those who place their trust in Jesus. Jesus took the curse of sin that plagued our spiritual accounts and hung on the cross as the payment for that sin.[15] He was a substitute payment for us— what theologians call *substitutionary atonement*. This one act, as Romans 5:18 says, "resulted in justification and life for all people." Friend, this should send chills down our spines and fill our eyes with tears. May we never grow numb to the truth that Christ Jesus loved you and me passionately enough to humble himself to take the form of a man and die on the cross a death he didn't deserve, all so he could redeem us. All that to get back the garden-like relationship that had been lost in the Fall. So see how the cross reverses the Fall? We can't properly understand the cross without Creation or the Fall. Again, these layers of

---

14. Galatians 4:6; Romans 5:5; Ezekiel 36:26–28; John 14:17.
15. Galatians 3:10.

the story build off each other.[16] Best of all, it is done for you and me.

Redemption is a part of our hermeneutic because while we understand all too well that this life is plagued with sadness, loss, and grief, we also understand that God did not stand far away, keeping himself separate, but instead chose to stand with us amid life's sorrows.

While you're reading the Bible, it's important to see how everything shifts with Redemption. All four gospels head full speed toward the cross. Through various literary elements, each of the Gospels has at its pinnacle the death and resurrection of Jesus and ends with the ascension and Great Commission. They lead us by hand toward the cross, taking us through the resurrection and ascension and leaving us asking ourselves some important questions: *Will I follow? What do I do now? What do I believe now? Will I share it?* Then the rest of the New Testament breaks down what Redemption means for life, death, worship, and glory.

I like to picture Redemption as the door hinge of the Bible. The tighter the hinge closes, the easier the door can close into place and lock. The cross's redemption isn't a weird curve-ball God threw into the storyline to mix everything up. It fills a cross-shaped hole in the story of redemption; it is exactly what was needed. We need to understand Redemption properly in order to understand the rest of the Bible. If we don't, both the New Testament and the Old Testament will seem confusing— and the metaphorical door to our house will be left wide open,

---

16. This doesn't mean that if you are a new believer, you can't start out reading the Gospels first, but it does mean that we see in the Bible how our systematic theology is based on these developing layers of the biblical story.

allowing any kind of false doctrine to wander in. Redemption, as the hinge, keeps the door tight and closed against false doctrine. Jesus is the door[17]—and the Way—but you can't understand how he is the Way without first understanding what he fulfilled.

The Final Restoration to a Better Garden: The Consummation[18]

The final piece of the storyline is the hope we have as believers who have entrusted our faith and our lives to Jesus. The Consummation is the final righting of all wrongs. While we live in the now and not yet—which is a theological phrase describing the fact that we have the benefits of the cross now but sin will not be completely defeated until heaven[19]—the Consummation is the complete renewal of creation and reversal of sin. It's illustrated in Revelation 21–22 as the new heaven and new earth, where every tear will be wiped away and sin will be no more. The Consummation is the culmination of the plan of God.

---

17. John 10:9.

18. Remember, this is often a word we use exclusively to refer to a romantic relationship and sexual intercourse. In the context of a contract, however, it means that all the requirements of the contract have been completed. Theologically speaking, this is the idea we have in mind. Consummation is when the promises have been kept, everything is complete, and we have the close, intimate relationship with the Lord that is better than what any sexual romantic relationship could bring.

19. My son Win recently asked his Sunday school teacher why there is still sin if Jesus said it was "finished." Friend, we are living in mere moments of grace. Though we are finite and time bound, these moments we have are for the ransoming of souls. Praise the Lord that this is where we are, because we still have time to herald the good news. The Lord has graciously given us this time to beckon our neighbors living and dying in sin to the Lord. When the final Consummation comes, there will be no more battle; it will have been fully won against sin, death, and the grave. While we are righteously eager for the new heaven and new earth, don't miss our calling. We are to be busy proclaiming the gospel message!

At the Consummation, the battle against sin, death, and the grave will be complete. Though Christ fully paid for our sin on the cross,[20] the effects of sin on creation will be completely washed away and we will live in our resurrected bodies in this new heaven and new earth because of the work of our resurrected Savior. Figure 4.2 shows how Revelation 21:1–7 reads.

Revelation 21:1–7

Holy dwelling place of God with his people

Undoing of the curse of the fall.

We moved from a garden to a city!

[1] Then I saw "a new heaven and a new earth," for the first heaven and the first earth had passed away, and there was no longer any sea. [2] I saw the Holy City, the new Jerusalem, coming down out of heaven from God, prepared as a bride beautifully dressed for her husband. [3] And I heard a loud voice from the throne saying, "Look! God's dwelling place is now among the people, and he will dwell with them. They will be his people, and God himself will be with them and be their God. [4] "He will wipe every tear from their eyes. There will be no more death or mourning or crying or pain, for the old order of things has passed away."

Reversal of being cast out of the garden, and fuller completion of the incarnation

Notice these are all things attributed to the old ways.

[5] He who was seated on the throne said, "I am making everything new!" Then he said, "Write this down, for these words are trustworthy and true."

[6] He said to me: "It is done. I am the Alpha and the Omega, the Beginning and the End. To the thirsty I will give water without cost from the spring of the water of life. [7] Those who are victorious will inherit all this, and I will be their God and they will be my children."

This is our promised hope!

The hope we eagerly await and look forward to also shapes the way we understand the world and Scripture. We see so many fulfillments in just those seven verses alone. We see there is a new heaven and a new earth in verse 1, which references back to the Creation narrative and God's sovereign rule and control over it all. There is no longer any sea, which is often viewed as an

---

20. John 19:30.

uncontrollable force that snatches life away and attacks the weak. There is no longer any threat of the uncontrollable, because our God is now on the throne and has reconciled all things to himself. We also see there is a city. Because there used to be a garden, we might think we need to return to the garden, but no—now it is a city. It has developed. It is now full of the "bride of Christ" (Christians) because we have done our "homework" from Matthew 28:19–20 and shared the good news of the gospel of Jesus Christ.

There is also a voice, like one might expect at a coronation or a formal assembly, announcing the communion (close, redeemed relationship) with God and man (Rev. 21:3). In the incarnation of Jesus we saw this in part—Jesus humbling himself to the form of a man to live and die for our ransoming. We saw this also in part at Pentecost as the Holy Spirit fell on believers (Acts 2:1–4). But now it's closer than ever before: inside us. Now we see that the holy city is one in which God dwells. There is family unity, community, and security. Revelation 21:4 speaks of a security that responds to the aches of our earthly experience, an end to our tears and our pain because "the former things have passed away" (ESV). This is a reference to the Fall, which has plagued the earth since Eve's first bite of the forbidden fruit.[21] Then in verse 5 we are comforted that God is making all things new.

There is this cosmic reversal, which was initiated at the cross, coming to fulfillment here in the Consummation—the goodness of God swallowing up the evil of sin. In Revelation 21:6 we learn of God's sovereign decree guaranteed for those of

---

21. Romans 8:22.

us who are his, which is something that echoes Jesus' words in John 7:37–38. Waters of life. The thirst of our souls,[22] which we sometimes attempt to quench with money, acceptance, or happiness, is met in him. Bubbling over, spilling out, our cup overflows[23] with his satisfaction like a cold glass of water after a long, hot day of working outside.

The Consummation is a response to the rest of the Bible. You can't get it without the cross, though some attempt to adopt the hope of heaven and leave Jesus behind. The truth is that you can't have the hope of heaven without understanding the depth of the consequences of the Fall. You can't fully grasp the hope of the new heaven and the new earth without under-standing the sovereignty of our Creator God in the Creation narrative. Creation, the Fall, Redemption, and Consummation are all interconnected. When the Bible speaks about heaven, it's building off the lost garden from Creation, because of the sin and sorrow from the Fall, and bought by the work of Christ in Redemption. The opposite is true too. Just as the rest of the Bible is building off Creation, it is also pointing forward to Consummation (heaven). The rest of the Bible is pointing to our need for heaven, leaving little clues and hints of what's needed in a Messiah to get that redemption and how he will do it.

The Consummation also informs how we live today as those redeemed awaiting heaven. In light of the final Consummation, which we await, we must understand that we are really just strangers and aliens in this lost world, and our true citizenship is in heaven.[24] If we rightly understand Creation, the Fall, and

---

22. See John 4:14.
23. Psalm 23:5.
24. Hebrews 11:13.

Redemption, we will realize we weren't created for this world, along with the sin that plagues us every day, and that is why nothing satisfies us. The Fall is the emptiness inside of and around us, the cross ransomed us, and heaven is the home we are seeking.

Rightly holding our hermeneutic of Creation, Fall, Redemption, and Consummation, we now see that the Bible lays out this story not as a clue book so we can just find out what job to take or what person to date and move on with our lives but as a story much bigger than just you and me. The Bible is the story of God redeeming his people for his glory, and it is a story that (praise God) isn't finished yet.

Bible Nerd Notes

1. **RECAP.** Remember, our hermeneutic of the Bible as the story of God redeeming his people for his glory can be broken down into four parts: Creation, the Fall, Redemption, and Consummation. These terms are not given to you to complicate your reading but as a framework to simplify and help you understand the Bible, summarizing it into one cohesive story so you can break it down into bite-size pieces. Notice how I gave application for our lives from each chapter, but each chapter wasn't about us, it was still all about God.

2. **REFLECT.** Consider Matthew 28:18–20. Commonly referred to as the Great Commission, these are the last instructions of Christ spoken after his resurrection and before his ascension to heaven. Jesus calls on his authority over heaven and earth (v. 18), which reflects the authority of the Father at Creation.

Then Jesus commands his followers to make disciples of all the nations (v. 19), which reflects back to God's promise in Genesis 12:1–3 that Abraham would be a blessing to the nations, despite the Fall (pointing to Redemption). Then they are called to baptize in the name of the Father, the Son, and the Holy Spirit, teaching the redemption of Jesus Christ and the good news of salvation. Then Jesus declares that he is with them always, implying that garden-like intimacy has been restored. This anticipates the fullness of relational closeness to be restored in the Consummation. Through every page of the Bible, we see that the story of the Bible is one that moves from Creation to Consummation, and we see references to each of these chapters along the way, forming our theology.

3. **COMPARE.** Creation, the Fall, Redemption, and Consummation give us, like chapters in our favorite book, a framework to help us understand how the story of God redeeming his people for his glory evolves. That's why the New Testament can feel different from the Old Testament. God hasn't changed, but the Old Testament was written from the perspective of the Fall looking forward to the cross and Redemption. Then the New Testament reveals that anticipated Redemption. Consider writing this in the table of contents inside your Bible. Every book listed as part of the Old Testament points forward to our need for redemption, and every book listed in the New Testament explains Redemption while looking forward to Consummation. It should transform our reading of the Bible to know that all of God's Word is looking forward to heaven. Even more, it should affect the application of Scripture to our lives because the story isn't over. In fact, the story is still going. How will you live in it?

CHAPTER 5

The Big Picture

Next to our house is a patch of woods with a creek that my family and I adore. We prayed to find a house with woods and a creek that our boys could play in, and God chose to grant us that prayer request in his sheer kindness. On hard days, when the emails pile up and research is weighing me down, I step outside to walk among the most beautiful trees in all of Texas (I'm biased). It's like I've stepped into C. S. Lewis's Narnia and all my problems have disappeared. Maybe it's the fresh air, the sun warming my skin, or the illusion of twinkling lights as the sun glimmers through waving tree branches, but something exceptional happens when I head outdoors. There, I can forget about my computer and the piles of laundry that need to be folded. The woods are my sanctuary where I am reminded that I am just a small creature in this big story God's working out. Though five minutes ago the mountain of emails made it feel like my whole world was boiling over, in reality emails are nothing in the larger scope of life.

Similarly, Scripture makes more sense when we take time to step back and see the big picture. Just as I occasionally need to step out of my office and into the woods to reorient myself, I encourage you to step back and look at the big-picture storyline of God's Word.

The Storyline of the Bible

By rightly understanding Creation, the Fall, Redemption, and Consummation, we can see the full storyline of the Bible (fig. 5.1). This enables us to know where we have been and see where we are going, no matter which part of the Bible we are reading. If it is before the cross, it points to Jesus in some way. If it is after the cross, it unpacks what the cross means for us today. If it is before the Fall, it is setting the scene for the Fall.

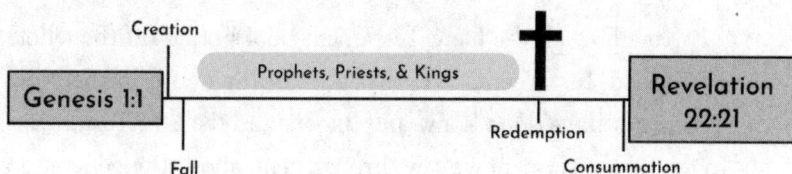

Every time I read the Bible, I mentally scan this chart and ask myself, "Where am I reading?" If I am in the Old Testament, the passage is looking forward to Jesus, the cross, Redemption, and Consummation (fig. 5.2).

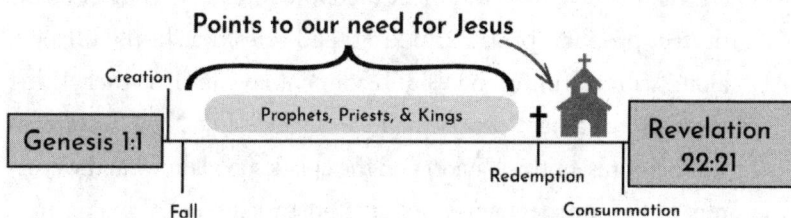

If I am in the New Testament, it's likely that whatever I am reading is explaining or revealing the work of Jesus on the cross (fig. 5.3). This can be through explaining our theology, worshiping, living, and awaiting Jesus' return. One clarifying point: If I am in the Gospels, these four books are in the New Testament right before Redemption. They are setting the scene for the cross and ending with Redemption.

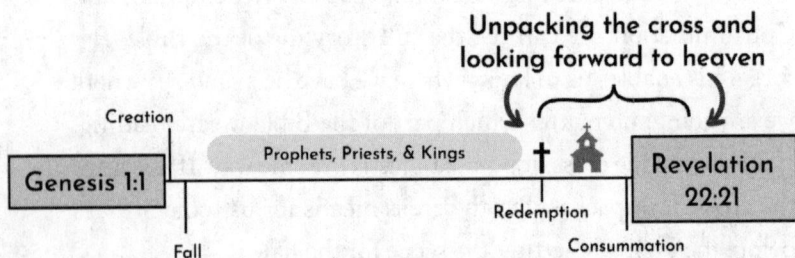

Note how all the New Testament books build off the whole of the Old Testament. We miss a lot of the depth in the New Testament if we don't know and understand the Old Testament. In the Old Testament we saw through generation after generation the depths of the Fall. Though people back then did have the law, it didn't always solve every problem—we read about Moses' doubt, David's adultery, and Solomon's insatiable lust. The New Testament books build off the Old Testament, which displayed through every prophet, priest, and king our need for a Savior, the Messiah. The New Testament therefore reveals this Savior as the perfect prophet, priest, and king—all roles that Jesus fulfilled, along with fulfilling the Old Testament law. Jesus is everything the Old Testament proclaimed we needed. The New Testament Gospels present this Savior, and the epistles explain what the cross means for our theology, worship, and anticipation of his return.

While you're reading God's Word with this storyline in mind, keep an eye on not only where the book of the Bible is going but also where it's coming from. Genesis 4 is shaped by Creation and the Fall, and is awaiting Redemption and Consummation (heaven). Second Timothy is informed by Creation and the Fall just as much as it is shaped by Redemption. The Gospels are the start of the New Testament, revealing the Messiah, so they are testifying of his message, work, and atoning sacrifice. But the majority of the text of the Gospels takes place before the cross and spends much of the time building up to it. It is therefore *not* going to deal with as much theology. That is what the rest of the New Testament focuses on. The Gospels were written to reveal the Messiah. They are testifying of who Jesus is, what he did, and what he said. The rest of the New Testament wrestles with the "now and not yet," which is the waiting and looking forward to heaven (Consummation) but also enjoying the change that God is doing in us and the church in the meantime.

I hope you see now that Creation, the Fall, Redemption, and Consummation frame the way we view the Bible as a whole. They also inform the way we read each individual book of the Bible. They give us a way to understand the function and use of each book of the Bible. They are not necessary,[1] but they are incredibly helpful.

---

1. I am not saying you need to understand Creation, the Fall, Redemption, and Consummation in order for God to work through Scripture in your life. Rather, it is a framework God has established in his story that benefits our conception of his redemptive plan. I also find that when I teach this framework of the Bible, it helps many students of the Word to understand and see the unity of the New and Old Testaments. This framework is not something I came up with, nor is it something that "works" in only one denomination, but rather it is something that traces back through the church to theologians such as Irenaeus and Augustine of Hippo. Though some denominations and traditions teach it more than others, it is Christian in nature, not denominationally specific. It is a helpful framework for every Bible-reading Christian's hermeneutic.

CFRC's Impact in Bible Study

The ability to understand the grand scope of Scripture is a major need in our churches, Bible studies, and Sunday school classes today. Many Christians spend far too long, maybe even the majority of their lives, feeling lost in the grand narrative of God's Word. They may flip open the Bible to Jeremiah 3 and read it having no idea what led up to Jeremiah being compiled and why it matters to us today. With a quick glance, however, most Christians can figure out that Jeremiah is in the Old Testament and therefore comes before the cross and Redemption (fig. 5.4).

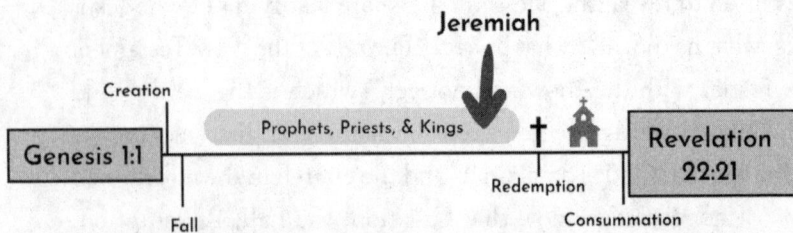

Knowing that Jeremiah was written after the Fall but before the cross shows us that it is dealing with sin and the consequences of the Fall but is awaiting the Messiah. We should read Jeremiah knowing that it is before the cross, and therefore it is pointing to our need for the cross. It is pointing to Jesus. It also is highlighting the importance of the role of a prophet, which is a role in the Old Testament that Jesus fulfilled. Jesus is the *perfect* prophet, priest, and king.

This is by no means everything that must be understood to study Jeremiah. It is, however, an example of how understanding the timeline of Creation, Fall, Redemption, and Consummation can get you started in understanding any book of the Bible. A student studying Jeremiah will also need to spend some time understanding Jeremiah's role, the exilic history, and the divided kingdom's demise. But understanding that Jeremiah happens before the cross and therefore points to Jesus is the first step toward this. Remember, the Bible is a story. It contains context, setting, a narrative arc, and an ending. All of the Bible is inter-textually connected and speaks to the movement of the grand story, from the garden of Eden to the heavenly city.

The Story of the Bible Is a Literary Masterpiece

I think those who miss the literary richness of the Bible miss a lot. The inverse is also true. But I say this because those who boil the Bible down to just a spiritual guidebook and refuse to acknowledge the literary form of Scripture are depriving them-selves of the richness of God's Word. It is not just a story, but it does work through the means of literature and literary elements. This is because God hardwired us to respond to story. When I began posting videos on the internet, I noticed which videos reached more people than others, and the common theme among my most successful videos was that the videos presented a story.

How could some viewers watch a thirty-minute makeup tutorial but not make it through a ten-minute Bible study? The answer was story. It didn't matter whether someone was making the silliest video ever (like "How Long Does It Take to Saw Through a Table with a Plastic Knife?" by Mr Beast); if there was a clear character, with a goal and an obstacle, the video would resonate with its audience much more than an easy sit-down-and-talk-to-the-camera kind of video.

I have finally learned to frame each of my videos as a story. I am the character who wants to have an in-depth Bible study, and my obstacles have included my children's limited nap time, a challenging passage of Scripture, or having only one single Bible study resource to use—that kind of thing.

While I am not changing reality (it is true that I want to give viewers an in-depth Bible study within the time limits of my children's nap time), I am transforming the way I communicate the information. This creates more tension in the viewers' minds, and they want to see the problem resolved. Now they're not just wondering, "How will she do it?" they're also asking themselves, "Can she do it before her children wake up?"

When I first started using this technique, I didn't go viral, but my videos did naturally start resonating with people a tad bit more. Our minds were created to feel and respond to the tension present in a good story. After all, we've been swimming in it ever since the Fall. We were created to love story. God created our brains to love story.

That's why the Bible is written as story. I also believe we find the most purpose and fulfillment in life when we realize we are all part of this cosmic story. We are all small but important characters in this Creation, Fall, Redemption, and Consummation narrative.[2] Our goal is to run the race set before us with our eyes fixed on the heavenly city with its tearless golden streets.[3] Yet every day we face obstacles and trials. And every day our King delivers us, carries us, and provides for us,

---

2. We are not the main characters. The Bible isn't about us. It is for us.
3. Hebrews 12:1–2; Revelation 21:4.

as he will do in the final chapter when the battle is completed and Satan meets his eternal fate.

I hope you see that the Bible isn't a rule book, a treasure map, or a set of riddles to be solved. The Bible is the story of God redeeming his people for his glory. The good news is he has already done that in you and me, is doing that daily in the church, and will continue to do it until the last chapter—our happy ending, the final Consummation. Praise the Lord for that! Glory be.

Bible Nerd Notes

1. **INVESTIGATE.** What is your favorite book of the Bible? Look back at the storyline of the Bible and find where it falls. Consider how your favorite book is affected by Creation, the Fall, Redemption, and Consummation. In what ways is it looking forward to the Consummation? In what ways is it informed or affected by the Fall? Does it point to Jesus or reveal what Jesus' work on the cross means for us today?

2. **RECAP.** Jesus fulfills the roles of prophet, priest, and king in the Old Testament. This means every time we read about a prophet, priest, or king in the Old Testament, it is looking forward to our perfect prophet, priest, and king: Jesus. This might sound weird, but notice how the New Testament makes that clear. Flip in your Bible to Matthew 21:11, highlight the word *prophet*, and write in your Bible margin: "Jesus is the final, perfect prophet!" (See also John 4:19; Heb. 1:1–2.) In Luke 1:32–33, highlight the words *throne*, *reign*, and *kingdom*. Write in the margin: "Jesus is the eternal King of our heavenly kingdom!" (See also Rev. 7:10;

19:16.) Read Hebrews 7:15–28, highlight verse 24, and write in the margin: "Jesus is our great High Priest with himself as the final sacrifice!" (See also Heb. 4:14; 9:11–12.)

3. **USE.** Consider making a copy of the storyline chart and turning it into a bookmark for your Bible. The next time you feel lost in your Bible reading, find where you are on the storyline, then ask how it is pointing forward to Jesus (in the Old Testament) or unpacking the work of Jesus (in the New Testament).

CHAPTER 6

Studenthood

One of my favorite books growing up was *Chain Letter* by Ann M. Martin, which was part of the *Baby-Sitters Club* series. This book was a collection of letters and notes passed among a group of friends and was made to feel "scrappy," which really inspired and intrigued me. There were envelopes to open and notes to read, photos and stamps to look at, and cards to unfold. I loved opening the envelopes and pulling out the letters—it made me feel like I was part of the story, and I think this was what inspired me to tape envelopes and pockets into my Bible!

Ann M. Martin could have written this children's book with just words. Instead, she chose to use letters, newspaper articles, and notes to tell the story in a real-life way (especially for that era).

We don't always see our stories lived out in a linear direction, with only the pertinent information given. Every day we face all sorts of microdecisions, receive a variety of information, and have different interactions with others, and all of these moments help build the stories of our lives. But we never realize what was important or life-changing until we look back on it all. This children's book reminds me of that. In that book we were given letters between best friends, newspaper clippings, and Polaroid photos, and we found the core story along the way.

Similarly, the Bible also tells its story through different forms of literature and from different points of view. Amid the story of Creation, Fall, Redemption, and Consummation, we come across poetry between two lovers (in Song of Solomon), horror stories of the judges[1] (in Judges), and warnings of the prophets (in Isaiah and Jeremiah, for example).

No matter where you are in the Bible, amid the story of God redeeming his people for his glory, you are also in a specific book, which falls into some form of literature. That's why the Psalms are usually so much easier to understand than Isaiah. There are many different genres of literature in the Bible, and each genre is supposed to be read in a certain way. All of these genres require us to partake in a certain level of "studenthood" to know what we are reading and what to expect from them. But surely at this point in the book you know that getting nerdy about the Bible is quite fun.

If you've been on the internet for any amount of time, I'm sure you can think of a million examples of different genres online. A tweet shouldn't be read in the same way you read a medical research article. A Facebook post written by Uncle Billy Bob shouldn't be taken as seriously as a news article (and knowing Uncle Billy Bob, it's probably fake news anyway).

---

1. Shout-out to Andrew Judd, who labeled the book of Judges as horror literature—and has rocked my world ever since. This has totally transformed the way I read Judges. See Judd, *Modern Genre Theory: An Introduction for Biblical Studies* (Grand Rapids, MI: Zondervan Academic, 2024), 107–16.

Jokes aside, we consume all sorts of literature throughout the day and understand that they should be consumed in different ways—whether school textbooks or text messages or love letters. No one needs to tell us that text messages aren't as serious or factual as the news headlines that pop up on our phones. We know this because of culture, experience, and past interactions with these types of communication. In the same way, the people of the ancient Near East and the first century had certain expectations for different literary forms, such as gospels, parables, and wisdom literature.

When we pick up the Bible, however, we are picking up ancient pieces of all types of literature that we don't have much experience interacting with. To make it even more challenging, they are all bound into one book, which seems to tell our brains that we should read all of it the same. While we spent time in chapters 3 through 5 learning about the unity of the Bible's story, I also want you to know that different types of literature form that story.

The Bible uses the types of literature we are used to in our modern culture, but it also includes genres that seem foreign to our modern worldviews. Some of this literature might seem pointless to us today—for example, genealogies that don't lead to the birth of Jesus or records that don't prioritize precise measurements or dating. But God chose to tell the story in this specific way through these human authors, despite their finitude and because of his infinitude. Despite the confines of culture and the limits of language, God continues to work through this ancient document, because it isn't just an ancient document, it is the living Word of God[2] that still has the ability to change us every day.

---

2. Hebrews 4:12; 2 Timothy 3:16–17.

Popular Misconceptions About the Bible's Literature

Most people open the Bible assuming it was written with a linear timeline, like a modern-day story, with one character who will teach us something. You may have gotten that idea from my previous chapter where I discussed the unity of Scripture. But the unified narrative of Scripture is formed through different genres and recorded through various historical periods, sometimes by unknown authors.

Sometimes the story retells itself,[3] and at other times the same story is told from another point of view.[4] Much of the Bible was originally consumed aurally, because the printing press was not invented until AD 1440.[5] The Bible was recited and read aloud to congregations of people for longer than we've had it in print. It is a new concept to read God's Word on our own, enjoying the quiet of the morning while drinking a warm cup of coffee. I say all of this because it's important to remember that the Bible was originally intended for public conviction rather than personal consumption.

Think about how it would change the way you view and interpret the Bible if it was shared only with congregations that contained large masses of people. Imagine the way the David and Goliath narrative would be transformed if you didn't read it by yourself but instead you were listening to it being read to a crowd of four thousand souls as you were in exile in a foreign land (when you'd lost everything and it felt like God didn't care

---

3. See, for example, Genesis 2 retelling what already happened in Genesis 1.
4. See, for example, the retelling of parts of 2 Samuel and 1 and 2 Kings in 1 and 2 Chronicles. Chronicles serve as a sort of retelling after the exile instead of before or during.
5. The printing of the Bible was AD 1455.

about you anymore). Imagine how much less you'd be thinking about yourself as you listened to the story, and how you'd be thinking more about God and how he works in, through, and despite circumstances to redeem his people for his glory. You wouldn't be asking how you could be like David and wondering what your Goliaths were, because the focus wouldn't be on you. Instead, you'd be thinking about the narrative on a much wider scale in view of the community of God's people.

We live in a culture and time where our worlds can exist next to each other but barely cross. I'm a good example of this. I avoid the news like the plague. I haven't talked to my neighbors in probably more than a month, yet they live within walking distance of my front door. I haven't willingly struck up a conversation with a stranger in months, excluding regular interactions at stores and in restaurants. I love my bubble! I *hide* in my bubble! In my bubble, the world revolves around me and my family, which is quite nice.

But we weren't created for this individualistic existence, and the ancient Near Eastern peoples whose stories are told in our Bibles didn't live like this either. They not only were closely dependent on their neighbors and community but also didn't see themselves as existing for self, as we do today. They didn't have their own social medias, such as Instagram or TikTok. They didn't even have their own rooms! Their survival was heavily dependent on the survival of the community. Their identity was defined by their community and their family. Yes, they were still selfish sinners, but their culture was structured to be less self-centered than ours is today. Therefore, if we read our self-centered perspectives into the Bible, we are missing what the original authors intended in their messages.

At this point you might be wondering, "Faith, how do you know what the original authors intended?" This is something I get asked every time I teach online about treating the biblical text as it was intended to be treated, so you are not crazy to wonder this. It is a critical part of our studenthood. As with other types of literature, we sometimes know the intended purpose of the text because it is clearly stated,[6] but most of the time we know the purpose by examining the authorship and dating and determining how it was used throughout the rest of the Bible. I mentioned the David and Goliath narrative, recorded in 1 Samuel 17. This book probably was compiled during the exile from earlier narratives authored by Nathan, Gad, and Samuel. First Samuel was compiled during the exile to remind God's people about their identity, the covenant promises, and the character of their God.

Imagine getting pushed out of the holy land—including God's holy city—being captured, and seeing your homeland destroyed. When you look around at all that's happened, it's easy to wonder why your God has abandoned his people. Then you hear the story of David, the great king who was used by God to defeat a strong, threatening nation with a rock, a slingshot, and a huge heart of faith. While you look around at this pagan nation that has taken you captive, saying that their god Marduk must be greater than your Yahweh, you are reminded by David's story that God's people have always faced threatening forces. God's people have always been mocked. But God has always used even the smallest amount of faith for his purposes. And when you look around at the congregation of God's people, you feel the mutual conviction.

---

6. See John 20:31.

After years of worshiping both Yahweh and the pagan gods of the lands around you, you hear the words David said to the scary Philistine giant: "This day the LORD will deliver you into my hands, and I'll strike you down and cut off your head. This very day I will give the carcasses of the Philistine army to the birds and the wild animals, and the whole world will know that there is a God in Israel. All those gathered here will know that it is not by sword or spear that the LORD saves; for the battle is the LORD's, and he will give all of you into our hands."[7]

You and everyone you know have normalized this doubt of Israelite monotheism. You and everyone you know have started to question Yahweh entirely. But now you feel the Spirit start to wiggle inside you. The stories you've heard don't feel like stories; they make you feel as though you belong to the most powerful God in all of history. You realize that maybe the judgment Goliath took for the mockery of Yahweh reflects the judgment God's people are facing in exile for their similar mockery of Yahweh.

You and your people have faced horrible loss, but you are encouraged by hearing the truths of the David and Goliath story. There's no self-centered exegesis such as "God's going to help me face my Goliaths!" Instead, the focus is on God's almighty power that can work through even a rock and a sling. You're grateful for God's sovereignty and justice. You are comforted in God's mercy and steadfast love. But, more important, the more you think about David and Goliath, the "bigger" your view of God gets and the less you think about yourself. Maybe that is a good rule of thumb: A good exegesis of the Bible will

---

7. 1 Samuel 17:46–47.

not lead us farther into our self-centeredness but rather inspire us to worship.

Hopefully this gives you a small picture of how our reading of the text can be transformed when we keep in mind the original author, the audience, and the historical moment the text was written for. This doesn't mean the Bible can't be used in other circumstances or historical moments (it definitely affects them), but we'll have a richer and deeper understanding of the text when we read it in its correct historical context.

Why would we want to deprive ourselves of the richness of Scripture? Let's feast on the depths of the living and active Word of God by studying it for what it says, not what we choose to read into it.[8] When we look at the Bible's broader story and purpose, we will be led to worship our good and faithful God. We gain this when we consider not only the historical authorship and purpose of a book of the Bible but also how it was written to fit a specific cultural era or literary genre.

So Many Genres, So Much Rich Meaning

The Bible includes books that are written in many different genres, such as poetry,[9] apocalyptic literature, and wisdom literature. Additionally, within the books of the Bible are different types of literature. First Corinthians includes quotes,

---

8. This is what we identified as eisegesis back in chapter 3. For more on this, check out E. Randolph Richards and Brandon J. O'Brien, *Misreading Scripture with Western Eyes: Removing Cultural Blinders to Better Understand the Bible* (Downers Grove: InterVarsity Press, 2012).

9. Approximately one-third of the Old Testament is Hebrew poetry.

exhortations, and commands, and it's also rich with theology. These genre types are at times all mixed together in a book or passage and at other times there are clear divides.[10] Most important, each type or genre of literature needs to be understood and applied in different ways. When my husband texts me a sarcastic message, I get it, because I know his humor and I understand he means the opposite of what he's saying. That's the beauty and the struggle of the written word—we are always interpreting it, even when we're reading it at face value.

This is why I am not a fan of perpetuating the talk around a "literal" reading of the text. Some people like to say, "Well, I just read the Bible literally and follow what it says. I don't twist it!" But a literal reading still requires a level of interpretation. It seems misleading to highlight a "literal" reading of the Bible when we openly acknowledge there is both figurative and symbolic language throughout different genres.

Everyone knows God doesn't literally have wings in Psalm 91:4. No one (that I am aware of) who reads that verse insists that God has wings. Rather, they understand it's a metaphor of God's protection, calling to mind the image of a mother bird who wraps her wings around her vulnerable babies. All of us have our own interpretation of everything we read and hear. You are interpreting my words now as a break in the "fourth wall,"[11] reminding you you're reading a book. You are interpreting my words to be a little bit sassy and not at all joking (hopefully). Interpretation is a cognitive function that we can't just switch

---

10. For example, see how most translations separate the quote in 1 Corinthians 10:7 with quotation marks.

11. Breaking the fourth wall is when a character in a movie, show, or book directly acknowledges the audience, stepping outside the story as if they know they're in it.

on and off. The key is to be mindful of what our presuppositions are as we enter into reading God's Word. This is a critical part of our humble studenthood of the Bible. Ask yourself, "Am I assuming this is a metaphor?" Or "Am I assuming this is a suggestion when it's really a command?" We must also ask ourselves a series of questions as we read: "What am I expecting out of this text? Do I believe it is true? What is its purpose?"

There are numerous texts that people today read as literal; however, they were never intended to be read that way. For example, many newer or younger believers read Proverbs 31 as a set of rules for a godly woman—for example, "I must wake up before anyone else or else I'm not a good wife" (see v. 15)—when, in reality, many of the tasks listed couldn't possibly be done in the same season of life, let alone every day.[12] Furthermore, there are many things a good wife should do in addition to what is listed in Proverbs 31. The chapter simply gives us a picture of a wise woman, not the perfect wife. And many scholars argue that this text isn't intended for just women, men should also study and follow it. This is because Proverbs 31 isn't a set of rules or a list describing the perfect woman to marry but rather wisdom to be desired by all. That is the genre of wisdom literature. It was intended not as hard-and-fast rules but as a picture of what it means to truly be wise.

There are also numerous passages of the Bible that we skip over and don't read at all, because we misunderstand that the genre of literature is telling us something bigger than the words we read at face value. For example, Matthew's gospel starts with a genealogy. We might roll our eyes at the thought of finding

---

12. Compare verse 15 to verse 18: She stays up late but also wakes up early. That surely cannot happen daily for any long period of time!

anything of value in a boring genealogy, but Matthew includes it at the beginning of his gospel because he is attempting to show Jewish believers that Jesus really is the promised Messiah from the line of David who fulfilled all the prophecies.

Notice how these two examples, from Proverbs 31 and Matthew 1, hinge on the type of literature they are. The book of Matthew is a gospel—which is a first-person account, or testimony, written to believers to encourage them in their faith—and inside that gospel is a little moment of genealogy that provides further encouragement. Proverbs 31 is the final chapter in a book of wisdom that has used, over and over again, the metaphor of a certain woman's life to teach the lesson of what wisdom does and doesn't do. Throughout the book of Proverbs we read about a harlot (or "folly") calling out in the streets to allure passersby (9:13–18) and wisdom calling out to whoever will listen (1:20–33). Then the book of Proverbs ends with chapter 31, which illustrates the picture of a good wife, who is a godly woman, and describes what her life looks like.

Both Matthew 1 and Proverbs 31 are God's inerrant Word, applicable and convicting for our lives today, but interpreted outside of their genres, they might seem confusing or boring (or both). That's why understanding genre is so important. It deepens our understanding of Scripture.

I previously mentioned my husband and his sarcastic texts. What I didn't say is that he often jokes about the fact that no one understands when he's being sarcastic. He has realized that he has to be careful about who he's sarcastic around, because some people don't understand his humor and think he's being serious. They don't know his personality and aren't familiar with his style of communication, so it's understandable if they think he is being rude and walk away offended. But as his wife, married to him for a decade, I know his tone. I know him intimately, and I get his humor. I have studied his smirk and have learned to recognize the faint mischievous sparkle that appears in the corner of his eye when he's being sarcastic, and I can distinguish it from how he looks when he's being serious. This is because I know him. I've been studying him since the moment I laid eyes on him in the fall of 2013.

Similarly, we want to be students of the Word who aim to have the same sort of close relationship with the Bible. We need to know who wrote it, when they wrote it, and to whom they wrote it. We must know what to expect in the genre so we can see when it breaks form. We do all of this not as some weird religious hyperfixation but because we believe God's Word is true and we want to be faithful to it.

But Faith, How Do I Do That?

Let's address the elephant in the room: It's not that simple. This is all difficult because it is ancient literature we're talking about, with ancient understandings of genre. We have no idea what it feels like to be a Hebrew who listens to a story about God shared by memory for hours on end. We cannot relate to prophets walking around in sackcloth and ashes yelling about future events. So how are we to figure out literature, genre, and all of this background information? How are we supposed to understand all the intricacies of the Bible? Through *studenthood*—daily, faithful, conviction-filled study of the Bible.

Friend, if you're reading this book wondering whether you really have what it takes to be that kind of student of the Bible, let me encourage you that our studenthood is a journey that God initiates. Best of all, I'd argue he has already started you on that journey, and that's why you're reading this book. Let's run full speed ahead in this journey of studying the richness of his Word.

Bible Nerd Notes

1. **INVESTIGATE.** Read Exodus 15, the historical record of Moses' praise song after crossing the Red Sea. This song is mixed into historical narrative (the actual story part). There's no introduction that says, "You're about to read a song—take that into consideration!" Most translations make the song look visibly different by formatting it in stanzas, printing it in spaced-out poetic lines. But it goes beyond just how the words are printed on the page. This is an ancient Near Eastern victory praise hymn that uses themes, hyperbole, and elements from other songs—and the music of the day. How does this change the way you read it?

2. **COMPARE.** Compare Exodus 15:11–16 to Psalm 77:13–15. Then read Revelation 15:3 and see the influence of the song from Exodus 15 in even the praise of heaven. Notice that this isn't just a song. It was indeed sung and ought to be sung in our churches today, but it also formed Israel's theology throughout the rest of the Bible.

3. **REFLECT.** After looking at Exodus 15 and Revelation 15, reflect on the role of genre in our theology. As we enter into our study of genre, I pray we discover that every genre still plays a role in

---

our theology. My goal is that we realize nothing is *just* a song, a poem, a letter, or a story. It's all Scripture. Hold tight to this truth as we move forward throughout this book. God is moving and working through every paragraph, line, and word. It is all testimony of him redeeming us for his glory.

CHAPTER 7

Not Just a History Textbook

On Sundays my boys like to grab the crayons out of my Bible bag and color all over their church bulletins as my husband or other church leaders take the congregation through the announcements, prayer time, and liturgical introductions for our worship time. I delight in how my sons' precious drawings get better and better every week. What once were blobs have now become full-on human-looking creatures and tic-tac-toe games. I know that one day their drawings will turn into doodles, and maybe every once in a while they'll pass me a note that reads "Can I have some gum?" These days when their tiny fingers grip onto crayons as they draw everything in their imaginations are fleeting, so I'm doing my best to treasure them while they last.

One Sunday my oldest son, Winchester, who was learning to read, passed me a note very proudly. I opened it to see a classic drawing of the globe in green and blue and seven purple squiggled letters that read "God love." He was so proud of his creation, and I wondered when he'd learned to spell *love*. After giving him a thumbs-up, I thought about how precious it was that he understood God's love was for the whole world. But then I began to question myself. Is that really what he meant? Or did he mean God's love had created the world? Or did he mean that we take God's love to the world? Or was it possibly that God's love for us is bigger than the whole wide world?

I'm still confused to this day. What did he mean by those two powerful words? What was his intention? Either way I look at it, it is convicting and encouraging, but what *did* he mean? Maybe you feel this way about something Jesus said in the Bible. Maybe you feel that way about large chunks of the Bible. Either way, I can relate.

There are a lot of texts in the Bible that people use to argue multiple different things, sometimes even things that are in opposition. Most of the time we need to first understand the genre of the text before we can even start to discern the message. Is it a parable? Sarcasm? Not a command but a suggestion? These tough questions can be answered by determining the genre and diving into the use of the text.

While the next few chapters address the big, overarching genre types within the Bible on a book, chapter, or even paragraph level, there are genres inside genres in the Bible. Books of the Bible don't always stick to specific genres. Psalms can be laments or praises. The book of Acts gives church history as well as theology, and these literary forms are interwoven line by line.

We shouldn't look at distinctions in genre as strict lines or black-and-white groupings. We might be reading a historical narrative where someone in the text suddenly breaks into song. That's a different genre, and the switch tells us how we are to understand the bigger narrative. We can read seductive poetry between a woman and a man (in Song of Solomon) while at the same time see themes of rich theology. Genre overlaps, jumps around, and breaks rules.

If you google "genres in the Bible," it seems like everyone and their brother has a slightly different view or grouping. It is fluid and messy, much like genre today. My husband and I love the soundscape of country music while we drive down the dirt roads that lead to our house. We might totally disagree with the lyrics and lifestyles highlighted in some of these songs, but the Dobro just hits different. Lately, when we tune in to pop country, we're surprised to discover that artists like Post Malone have stepped into the country world. Does that mean that this song is R&B or pop now that Post is singing it? Of course not! He's just putting his own twist on a country song. Similarly, books I read sometimes quote songs, Scripture, or even movies, which is similar to the genres inside bigger genres that we come across in the Bible.

With that in mind, let's look at the seven big genres within the Bible, starting first with historical narrative.

Historical Narrative

Historical narrative is the classic story structure we find in the Old Testament and Acts. It is important to note that though we call it narrative, I like to specify it as historical not only to include classic history in this genre but also to affirm that it is indeed true, not made up. (Remember that even though I use terms like *text* or *character*, this doesn't mean that these stories are fictional.) Historical narrative makes up most of our favorite children's Sunday school lessons, including the Bible stories of Jonah, Noah, and Ruth—and of course David versus Goliath!

Historical narrative in the Bible is never just historical, because there is always a theological function. This means that all of these stories exist to inform the way we think and believe about God. Theological histories therefore tell only certain aspects of a story and prioritize things that we may not prioritize (because they are meant to inform our theology). This means historical narrative is not the equivalent of a modern-day history textbook.

In modern-day textbooks, history is retold to summarize events and share pertinent information, aiming to be as factual and precise as possible. Depending on the author or publisher, there might be a takeaway sprinkled into the chapter here or there, but it is not the purpose of the book to change the reader's life or the way the reader believes. The function and intent of the history textbook informs the treatment of the text. If you had a challenging history teacher like I did in high school (hey, Mr. Dorman!), you learned to skim-read the book and write down dates, locations, and names as if your life depended on it.

I don't know about you, but I didn't care about the author's life story. I probably never once thought about the people who wrote my textbooks because I was much more focused on passing tests and doing homework assignments. I didn't wonder about the author's favorite color or what he or she ate for breakfast. All I cared about was transferring information from the book to my brain so I wouldn't flunk out of Mr. Dorman's history class.

This is not how we should treat the Bible, though. The historical narratives in the Bible aren't just for the purpose of information transfer. That is one of the less important aspects of the text. The writers don't prioritize the facts or dates or locations but rather assume we are familiar with many of the places, customs, and events. For instance, the writer doesn't care about the exact number of people who were killed in battle, which is why most of the time the numbers are rounded into general approximations.

In fact, there is much to say about the big numbers we encounter in Kings and Chronicles. You can spend years studying the way the ancient Near Eastern people used large numbers and recorded kingly victories to form their desired reputation rather than record exact history. Much scholarship has been spent on their methods of recording history as a means of retelling the story the way they wanted it to be told. The ancient peoples didn't always have the same motives we have today when we record events.

I am not saying that the Bible isn't true. I am not saying that the narratives we have in Kings and Chronicles are exaggerated or only half-truths. I am saying, however, that it was cultural of the day and time not to look at the details but instead to look at the glory. Who was shamed and who was glorified? Which god won the nation's battle—Baal or Asherah? Who sounds like the more powerful god? Theology was their focus.

The Bible doesn't care about our twenty-first-century expectations of exactness. In our information-focused society, we can devalue a source if a date or location is shared incorrectly. But in the ancient Near East the focus was less on exactness of information and more on the bigger narrative: Where does your family belong? Who is the god of your people? What are your people known for?

Critics of the Bible love to find "contradictions" in God's Word and refute its reliability based on those supposed contradictions. But this is an anachronistic[1] approach to the Bible. Applying "rules" to the Bible that are not historically or chronologically appropriate is unfair. We know not to expect good CGI in the first Star Wars movies that were made, and we continue to watch—and enjoy—them, understanding that characteristically good CGI can't be expected from a product that was made in the 1970s. We also need to understand that numerical exactness and factual precision were not valued in many ancient Near Eastern contexts.

The narratives we find in the Bible are stories much like a modern-day testimony. These stories point to a general purpose. Genesis points to the establishment of God's people. Exodus shows their deliverance from slavery and moves the narrative into the establishment of a nation-state. The books (whose authorship is traditionally ascribed to Moses) answer a variety of questions: What is this people group? What is the meaning of the wilderness wanderings? Who is our God? Do we follow the most powerful God?

The narratives in the Bible share the testimony of our God and his people, and they point to Jesus through every prophet, priest, and king. This transforms our reading of the text because instead of thinking of these stories as just being about King Ahaz or Esther, we can also look for their theological messages. It was never really about Ahaz. It was—and is—always about our God who works in, through, and despite evil to ransom us to himself. Remember, the Bible is the story of God redeeming his people for his glory.

We'll miss the whole point of historical narratives in the

---

1. *Anachronistic* means we are using standards of a different time on a text. In other words, we are using modern rules or standards on an ancient text.

Bible if we reduce them to just stories about something such as a man building a boat and don't ask ourselves, "How is this informing my theology?" We'll miss everything if we don't pay close attention to the "extra" details the story shares for seemingly no reason. As students of the Bible who now understand this genre a bit better, we know that no information is shared that exists just as facts. It all informs the way we view God and the way he works.

Bible Nerd Notes

1. **INVESTIGATE.** Consider the beginning of the book of Ruth (fig. 7.1). Notice how the text starts by telling us it takes place during the era of the judges. (This was a time of low morality in God's people. Many describe the narrative of the book of Judges as a downward spiral because of how things were getting worse and worse.)

Era given! This means it must have been written after the period of the judges, probably during the kings, and it probably wants us to look forward to the kings.

Ancient people understood that famine meant their god was punishing them.

Signifies the start of a historical story

Ruth 1:1–2

City of King David, means "house of bread."

This name means "God is king."

¹In the days when the judges ruled, there was a famine in the land. So a man from Bethlehem in Judah, together with his wife and two sons, went to live for a while in the country of Moab. ²The man's name was Elimelek, his wife's name was Naomi, and the names of his two sons were Mahlon and Kilion. They were Ephrathites from Bethlehem, Judah. And they went to Moab and lived there.

Irony: A man whose name means "God is king" is leaving God's land, called the "House of Bread," because of a famine.

Uh oh! Why are God's people going to a foreign Canaanite god/land?

Starting the book by saying "Back in the day, when there were judges" tells us that this was written after the period of the judges. This means it was probably written in the era of the kings (and remember the great Israelite king David, from whose lineage comes our Savior). The first character mentioned, who is leaving God's land for the Canaanite land because of a famine, has a name that means "God is king." This narrative immediately has us asking in our hearts: "Do I live like God is king, or do I doubt him and flee?"

2. **REFLECT.** Notice the irony of a man leaving Bethlehem, which means "house of bread," during a famine. There is more going on here in the text than just a hungry man seeking food. The story is making some sort of theological point. (Remember, Bethlehem is the city of David and also where Christ was born. Also, in John 6:35, Jesus declares, "I am the bread of life.") Consider why the author chose to include this irony (leaving the house of bread for *bread*) and the theological point the author is making. One part of the text we might naturally skip over is "they were Ephrathites from Bethlehem, Judah." But this is the second time the author mentions they are from Bethlehem. Repetition is always important in the Bible! The author even uses unique phrases such as *Ephrathites* and *Bethlehem in Judah* to make it undeniably clear that these are God's people—and therefore people of promise—who are leaving God's land. Consider the theological impact that makes on this story. Instead of following the law and not intermarrying, the people are moving away and even marrying Canaanite women! They have seemingly lost their faith and trust in Yahweh as they are leaving the house of bread during a famine.

3. **RECAP.** In the Ruth narrative the information shared shows us the meaning of the text and its purpose. It's not just recording

history. We see how this narrative doesn't answer all our questions about this historical moment (such as we would find in a history textbook) but is focused on theology. Consider noting in your Bible what we discussed in the preceding paragraphs. For bonus Bible Nerd points, read all of Ruth and pay attention to what this narrative mentions regarding the famine, harvest, and barley. Notice how they come to Bethlehem just at the start of harvest (1:22) and how they end chapter 2 (2:23). Naomi came back to Bethlehem in chapter 1 "empty," but in chapters 2 and 3 Ruth's hands were full (see 2:18 and 3:17). The narrative includes these details on purpose to show us that even when we might declare we are empty (1:21), God's always providing above and beyond what we can expect, if only we will run to him—he truly is the bread of life (John 6:35).

CHAPTER 8

Not Just a Rule Book

One of the greatest thrills of childhood is making a good fort. Growing up, I made a lot of blanket forts, and yesterday my two sons made shipping-box forts for their stuffies that took up the entire living room floor. Using scissors, they cut doors and windows for their stuffed animals. They then made all sorts of furniture out of the cardboard scraps. Winchester's box fort looked like a bungalow cabin for his baby Yoda, and Sutton made an open-concept mansion for his elephant. They were pretty cool, and I have to admit I wanted to join in on making little items for the inside of these cardboard creations.

To secure their box forts, the boys used craft tape and were a bit disappointed that the tape wasn't working like they'd expected. I tried to explain to them that craft tape is different from shipping tape, which works better on cardboard. The box forts were really neat, but they weren't stable because the right kind of tape hadn't been used. Every time Yoda came through his front door, the roof opened up and the living room wall started to fall down because the tape wasn't stuck onto the cardboard.

Similarly, when many people read the Bible, they feel like nothing sticks together. Maybe the New Testament makes sense and feels comfortable, but the Prophets and their judgments seem like the gaping hole in the ceiling. The proper tape that holds all of God's Word together is, perhaps unexpectedly, the law. The law is the work of the cross, and the law is also the judgment of the prophets. So none of the Bible will hold together if we don't understand the law part. While this may seem at surface level boring or negative, I hope to transform your view of this essential part of the Bible. Because the law makes all the difference. Just like my boys didn't think about what type of tape would be best for their forts, we may want to skip over the law, but it's the tape that holds it all together.

The Law

One of the hardest parts of understanding the law is that it's often mixed with historical narrative, and it can be difficult to separate the two. The law is often our least favorite area of Scripture to spend time reading because it does not read like narrative. Rather, it includes tons of repetition and details about things that no longer seem to matter, and it's generally not very interesting (if we are being honest with ourselves).

But a core part of our theology of understanding the cross is understanding the law. The cross takes effect because of the law. We don't have *substitutionary atonement*[1] without the law.

---

1. This is the work Christ did through his life, death, and resurrection, which reconciles us to God. Jesus died in our place, taking the punishment for our sins and reconciling us to God.

We don't have the security of salvation through Jesus without the law. We don't have any benefits of the cross without the law.

Big picture: Christ fulfills the law to perfection.[2] But there is much more to say for all the detailed expanse of law in the Bible. As you may know, some of the laws in God's Word still apply to our lives today and other laws no longer apply.

Laws in the Bible are typically organized into three categories: *ceremonial law, judicial law,* and *moral law.* The tricky debate that spills into today is how to decipher what laws go into each category. At this point many authors would stop to define what each of these categories means. But I must point you to the fact that all law reveals God's character. His law gives us guidance in the ceremonial, the judicial, and the moral, but it also gives us so much more. The law is how God meets his people where they exist and showers them with love and provision. We miss everything if we just jump to categorizing the law into three groups and don't stop to see the heart of our God in the law.

Though the law at first might feel heartless and nonrelational, it is deeply personal and relational. I have never been a part of an adoption, but I imagine there is a point in the process in which a legal paper is signed. The relationship is sealed and ratified through a document that shows the change in status or relationship. The paperwork details the relationship between the child and the parents. It formalizes the transition of guardianship and outlines the change of status. Similarly, in the law we see the establishment of God's covenant relationship with his people. Because he is holy, this is how his children must live. This is where his house is located and how it is run.

---

2. Matthew 5:17.

The law is necessary for a holy God to have a people called to himself. The law is a necessary part of their consecration (being set apart as holy) and also is instrumental in the formation of a relationship between a holy God and sinful humans. This comes back to our understanding of the Fall. The law highlights the outworking of the Fall (sin) in our lives and it brings to light how costly the Fall was through the sacrifices required. It also looks forward to Christ as the one who will fulfill all the demands of the law in himself. As Israelites would cut the animal's throat and watch the blood (life) drain out, this was a very real symbol and reminder of their sins' devastating effects. Now that we are Christians atoned for by Christ's blood, however, this doesn't mean all the law needs to be thrown away or ignored. Rather, it shows us the kind of God we have and how he operates in this broken world.

The law establishes what it looks like to live as the people of God. Remember, the story of the Bible is the story of God redeeming his people for his glory. So while you read the law in the Bible—which is found in the Ten Commandments in Exodus, and in Leviticus, Numbers, and Deuteronomy—notice the clear directives for how God's people are supposed to live. They are to work together as a nation. They are to worship together. They are to hold moral convictions for the sake of justice. Through these moral, ceremonial, and judicial laws, God establishes a way of life ruled by his character.

Three Types of Law in the Bible

Keep in mind that while it's helpful to discern the three types of law that are found in the Bible (ceremonial, judicial, and moral), this threefold distinction is not something we find in the Bible or in the culture of ancient Israel. This is a modern solution to understanding what parts of the law apply not just to Christ's work on the cross but also to our lives today.

Ceremonial law points to Christ and his atoning work on the cross. These are the laws about sin offerings, temple worship, and food, all of which no longer apply directly to our lives today because Christ fulfilled them on the cross for us all. He was the final sacrifice. Since his work on the cross fulfilled the ceremonial law, we now read it seeing how it points to our need for Christ. And we can't read about this type of law without seeing how he fulfilled the demands of the law with himself. Because he was the final sacrifice, we no longer need to bring sacrifices in our worship.[3] He fulfilled the law around the temple so that we don't have to go into a church to draw near to his presence.[4] In fact, he brought the Holy Spirit to live inside us[5] so that he could be as close to us as possible, in our hearts. This is why gentiles[6] and Jews could gather together over the Lord's Supper—because the cleanliness laws had been fulfilled by Christ.[7]

When it comes to *judicial law* pertaining to the Hebrew nation, many understand this law to no longer apply except for the ways in which it shows equality, morality, and justice. It is important to see the role that judicial law played in the kingdom of God for a period of time, but it's also important to note that its weaknesses and insufficiencies show us the need for the eternal

---

3. Isaiah 53:5–6; Hebrews 10:11–14. Exception: Paul does entreat the Romans to offer their lives as living sacrifices in Romans 12:1–2.

4. John 2:19; 4:24.

5. John 14:26.

6. People who are not Jewish.

7. Acts 10:9–14; 15:5–11.

kingdom. Christ is the greater David. How is he king?[8] Christ is the eternal King (of his eternal kingdom), who rules and reigns in our hearts but also on a throne now, not established with human hands or threatened by war.

When it comes to *moral law*, most agree that it applies to all people, through all time. The morality established in the Old Testament is perfected in Christ and is to be lived out by his people. Moral law establishes the values and expectations of what it looks like to live as the people of God. We see through this type of law God's passionate heart for the poor, the widow, and the orphan, and also how he expects these values to be true of his people too.[9] So though Christ also met this law perfectly and completely, it is his morality that sets the pattern for how we are to live also.

I have to agree, in part, with scholarship that argues we should throw out these three distinctive groups of the law, because the law wouldn't have originally been viewed this way. I don't think the people of Israel sat around the table and debated what was moral versus what was ceremonial. It didn't matter to them. It was all law that needed to be followed. But as Christ followers who are redeemed by Jesus, it is important for us to ask, "Does any of this apply to us today?"

For example, some believers have questions about tattoos—is the Old Testament prohibition against them still applicable? Leviticus 19:28 prohibits cutting and marking your body for the dead, but does that apply to us today or was it only for ancient Israelites who may have been tempted to partake in pagan idol worship?. Questions like this may be relevant today,

---

8. Christ is the perfect prophet, priest, and king. So every time you see leadership in the Bible, whether it is positive or negative, it always points to Christ, who is the perfect leader.

9. See, for example, Deuteronomy 14:28–29; 15:7; 24:17–18.

but they're also secondary to salvation.[10] The most important question we need to ask ourselves is "Where is Christ in these laws?" Because he *is* there.

Not only is Jesus there in the law through shadows and fulfillments[11] but also he's there in his love and covenant relationship. The fact that God provided Israel with the law in order to have a relationship with them shows us that God seeks to redeem the broken relationship (broken at the Fall) with mankind. The law shows us that God is a God who seeks to ransom us to himself. Therefore, Christ is not hidden but rather evident through our need for the law. We should read the law and see the depths of our need for a Savior. Our hearts should groan, as the rest of creation does,[12] awaiting our Savior who will ransom us wholly to himself.

The law isn't text that no longer applies to us; the law is the means by which the cross applies to us. What do I mean by this? We have no salvation by Jesus' death on the cross if it didn't fulfill the law's demands. If he wasn't sinless, he wouldn't be the needed unblemished Passover Lamb.[13] Hebrews 9:23 and 10:4 tell us that the blood of bulls and goats wasn't enough—we needed something more, a fuller sacrifice that didn't just temporarily atone (until one sins again) but rather eternally saves.[14] We needed Christ, who fulfilled the law to its fullest extent with himself.

---

10. The rightful division of the Old Testament law is not something that saves or prevents salvation. This is what we refer to as *secondary issues*. There are some in the household of faith who would argue that the Old Testament laws prohibit modern-day tattoos and others who would say it does not, but both groups will be in heaven, as both have been saved by Jesus, not their right division of the law.

11. This means the law points to our need of Christ but also prophesies of Jesus.

12. Romans 8:22.

13. See Exodus 12:5–13 and 1 Peter 1:19.

14. See Wayne Grudem, *Systematic Theology: An Introduction to Biblical Doctrine* (Grand Rapids, MI: Zondervan, 2020), 705–51.

Most beautiful of all, we see God's love and justice on display in the law.[15] You might think I'm crazy to say that. It's literally law! No one looks at a courtroom and thinks, *Just the place I want to hang out!* But we have to remember that God's justice isn't like our earthly judicial systems, where a judge sits listening to evidence and witnesses while two lawyers yell at each other, aiming for their payday. True, good, biblical law is something created not out of the problem of sin but out of the fullness of goodness.[16]

Therefore, because God is both loving and just, he met the requirements of the law in himself. God, being all love and justice, is also loving and *gracious.* Those two realities of his grace and justice meet in his atoning work on the cross.[17] We should read the law in the Old Testament and see that God is providing not only a temporary means for atonement but also the very rule book he will meet with himself. He doesn't demand anything from his people that he doesn't demand from himself.

The Role of the Law in CFRC

Without the law showing us the role of the high priest and his work, we cannot understand the depths of the riches of Hebrews 2:17, which says: "He had to be made like his brothers in every respect, so that he might become a merciful and faithful high

---

15. For more on how the law participates in the larger story of redemption, I highly recommend Abner Chou's reflections in chapter 7 of *The Hermeneutics of the Biblical Writers: Learning to Interpret Scripture from the Prophets and Apostles* (Grand Rapids, MI: Kregel, 2018), in the section titled "The Use of the Law for a Believer," 215–18.

16. After all, there was law in the garden of Eden. See Genesis 2:17.

17. Romans 3:25–26.

priest in the service of God, to make propitiation for the sins of the people" (ESV). We cannot understand the feasts and Jewish holidays of the Bible without seeing how they are completed and fulfilled in Christ.

The law in the Bible is the outworking of the problem of sin meeting our just God who wants an intimate relationship with his people whom he is ransoming to himself. That is why law appears in our storyline after the Fall but before the cross (fig. 8.1). Remember what I said before about everything in the Old Testament pointing to our need for a Savior? We see this especially in the law. It, like the roles of prophets, priests, and kings, is a temporary role that is fulfilled (or met) eternally in Christ.

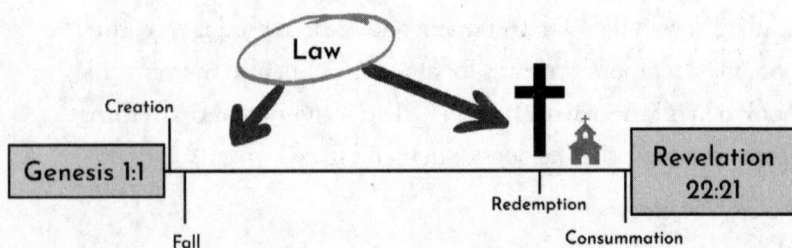

Friend, as you read various law passages in the Bible and are tempted to give up and skip over them, I encourage you to pause and ask yourself, "What does this passage reveal about God's heart?" Don't miss the depths of the riches of God's love and provision. Don't miss the Lamb of God meeting us in our depraved, law-bound sin. He meets us in our need, meeting the demands of the need *with himself*. Let his love wash over you as you read the law of the Lord, discovering his protection and provision in detailed accounts and explanations, and know that he cares.

Bible Nerd Notes

1. **INVESTIGATE**. Read Mark 7:1–23 and compare it to Leviticus 11. In verse 19, Mark writes that Jesus declares all foods to be clean. Does this mean that Mark is implying we skip over Leviticus 11 entirely now? Is he saying that the Pharisees were wrong for considering or valuing the law? No! Jesus clearly states in verse 21 that it is about the heart. Jesus calls us to a greater obedience to the law by enhancing the law, making it not about washing (what we can perform and do on the outside) but about where we place our trust (what we believe on the inside). Impurity is a heart issue, not a cleanliness issue. The Pharisees misunderstood Leviticus 11 when they didn't see that impurity was a heart issue, not just a physical issue.

2. **COMPARE**. Directly after Jesus' encounter with the Pharisees we just read in Mark 7:1–23, he moves on to seemingly break the law again in verses 24–30. Can you spot where this happens? Note what Mark mentions clearly for us in verses 25–26. When Jesus immediately goes to heal unclean gentiles, how does the gentile woman show a trusting, humble heart that was cleaner than the Pharisees' hands could ever be?

3. **REFLECT**. Finish our study today reading verses 31–37 of this same chapter. Jesus moves on to heal a man who was deaf. We see again how the Pharisees did not speak and hear the truth of Christ (because they were busy trusting in themselves), but the man who was deaf does, because he knows he is defiled, in desperate need of a Savior. Ironically, the man who was deaf "hears" the truth clearer than the Pharisees with the law.

Friend, may I encourage you: Don't have a pharisaical reading of the law that makes it all about rules of performance. If we
choose to read it that way, it is something we might as well skip
over, because Jesus has done it all for us. Instead, respond like
the man who was deaf, who realizes that at the heart of the law
is our desperate need for a Savior, because we cannot save ourselves. Respond to God today and call out to him in full reliance.

CHAPTER 9

Not Just a Letter

Last week while scrolling social media I came across a parenting hack. A mother explained that whenever she needs to ask her children to do something she thinks they won't do, she writes them a letter. She excitedly boasted, "When I write a letter, my child does what I ask every time!" She went on to describe an example of just how her method works. After she wrote her daughter a note asking her to clean up, it was like the young girl had temporarily been put under some sort of obedience spell. She read the letter, then raced off to pick up her toys. I couldn't help but wonder whether this would work with my boys. After all, my oldest son, Winchester, had just started reading and writing—and he could read the letter to his younger brother!

Whether it was about the toilet seat being left up or the pile of Legos covering their bedroom floor, there was always something I could ask my boys to do. I also wondered whether this letter-writing hack would work with chores. I was sick of reminding them to feed the goats. So I put my newly discovered parenting hack to the test. My husband and the boys were all taking a long nap, and I was downstairs working. I often don't hear them when they wake up, but my husband was exhausted from a long day of teaching and preaching and I wanted to make sure they would remain quiet so Daddy could keep sleeping.

I grabbed a piece of printer paper and wrote with a red colored pencil, "Dear Win and Sutt, Daddy is sleeping. Your mission is to play quietly in your room! Try not to wake Daddy up! And maybe clean up your toys!" I added some colorful washi tape to the note and taped it to their door so they wouldn't be able to open the door without seeing the note. I felt so clever. Maybe they'd really lean into this idea, play quietly, and even do some cleaning while I kept working on my book. A few minutes later Winchester walked into my office, groggy-eyed, and snuggled up onto my lap with the note in hand. Inside he had written back: "I'm too tired."

As funny as it is now, I really thought this hack would work on my sassy six-year-old and his younger brother. I share this story because this exemplifies how letters can be misunderstood, twisted, and disregarded.

The problem is that letters tend to be personal and contextualized. They are also bound to a specific culture, time period, situation, author, and recipient. The letter I wrote to my sons would not apply to my husband. It "works" only with children who are willing to accept the challenge, and it may be a cute keepsake, but it doesn't apply to all of time, like every time they wake up from a nap.

So why should we treat the letters in the Bible any differently? Why are letters in the Bible in the first place? It's important to understand that though there were many other letters written among the apostles and the early church, the letters, called epistles, we have canonized in our Bibles today are there because they are authoritative for all the church through all time. While there are verses that are highly contextualized and not particularly applicable today,[1] we can still see the heart of God in them and learn from an example of how we are to live to him.

As we move into the discussion of the epistles in the Bible, note how different these letters are from our modern-day messages. After all, as far as we know, the church never wrote back to Paul: "I'm too tired."

Epistles

Epistle is basically a fancy word for *letter*. That is why you'll typically find in an epistle a greeting,[2] a closing benediction,[3] and tons of references to real people,[4] locations,[5] relationships,[6] and previous conversations.[7] You'll find the epistles exclusively in the New Testament, and they are attributed to Paul, Peter, James, Jude, or John (plus whoever wrote Hebrews). It's notable that these letters were written by the apostles[8] to the early church.

---

1. See, for example, the focus on the collection in 2 Corinthians 8. This may not initially seem applicable to our lives, because it is bound up in a historic gift offering to a historic church in a time of need. But we can see godly generosity exemplified, and we can apply this same generosity to our own lives.

2. See Ephesians 1:1–2; Philippians 1:1–2; Colossians 1:1–2.

3. See Galatians 6:18; Ephesians 6:23–24; Philippians 4:23; Jude 24.

4. See 1 Thessalonians 3:6; Colossians 4:7–9; Philippians 4:2; 2 John 1.

5. See Titus 1:5.

6. See 2 Timothy 4:9; Titus 3:12; Philemon 10–16.

7. See 1 Corinthians 5:9; 2 Timothy 2:2; 2 Thessalonians 3:17.

8. These are people who have been sent by Christ to preach the gospel, and they are always those who have met Christ, with most having been his disciples.

These aren't random letters from Aunt Sally to Uncle Billy Bob. The Bible also doesn't include every letter the apostles wrote. These are the letters deemed authoritative for the church that have been shared, copied, and preserved (eventually leading to their canonization, to oversimplify it a bit). These letters held significant weight in the early church, and that is why they were passed around from church to church. The epistles, which are typically shorter in length than books such as Genesis or Psalms, are real documents that were written and read aloud to the church.

Letter Structure

It is important to study what the typical epistle framework looks like so we can note when an epistle breaks from the typical format. When they break from the expected pattern, it is always for a reason. For example, Galatians is known for its odd beginning. Instead of opening with a typical greeting and kind words like "Grace and peace to you," Paul jumps right out of the gate defending his apostleship. He says the letter was written by "Paul, an apostle"[9] instead of "Paul, a servant of Christ Jesus."[10] Typically, greetings were long and personal, but here Paul skips over a typical greeting so he can get right into theology. Also, typical greetings contained an acknowledgment of the author and the recipient, an extended greeting or blessing ("grace and peace"), and some type of thanksgiving ("I thank God for you"). Epistles also tend to have the same type of ending:

---

9. Galatians 1:1.
10. Romans 1:1.

a benediction,[11] an acknowledgment of the letter's authorship,[12] and any additional greetings that the author wanted to pass on.[13]

The acknowledgment of the person writing the greeting is notable, because often secretaries were used. These secretaries would do the writing, but their involvement in the recording of thoughts and choosing which words to use tends to be highly debated.[14] These secretaries had an unknown involvement in the authorship of the letters, but what we do know is that the letters were approved—and sometimes personally finished—by the author. Either way, no matter who was involved in which aspect of the letter writing, we can know that this is God's Word. Knowing this shouldn't challenge our view of the reliability or inerrancy of Scripture, because that is based on God working in, through, and despite us. The reliability of the epistles isn't dependent on who was behind the human authorship; the divine authorship is sovereign over every detail.

As you can see, there are many misunderstandings around letters and their historical origins that enter into our own readings of the epistles. While we understand a letter to be something that is fairly casual, there wasn't much casualness in these first-century letters that are now canonized in our Bibles. Because these letters were incredibly expensive to write and copy, their length alone is a visual and physical representation of the importance of the church receiving the gospel message. How would you feel if your church received a silver-plated letter

---

11. See, for example, 1 Thessalonians 5:23; Jude 24–25; Galatians 6:18.

12. See, for example, Galatians 6:11; 2 Thessalonians 3:17; Hebrews 13:22; 2 John 12.

13. See, for example, 1 Corinthians 16:19; Colossians 4:7–17.

14. For more on this, I recommend E. Randolph Richards, *Paul and First-Century Letter Writing: Secretaries, Composition and Collection* (Downers Grove, IL: InterVarsity Press, 2004).

from its founder, who happened to be an apostle who had met—and had been sent by—Jesus himself? It would be your claim to fame, and it would be read aloud over and over again—shared, memorized, and cherished by everyone in the congregation.

There wasn't much that could be considered casual about these letters, which were delivered by hand to their churches. They were then read aloud to the church and copied by hand for other churches to read. It's important to understand these details so that we don't belittle the choices the authors made. They were carefully composing well-thought-out letters about important topics that would be shared with many. These are not rushed text messages that would be quickly deleted and forgotten. When Paul rushed through the greeting in Galatians to get straight into defending the gospel, that was done on purpose. He didn't have time and money for niceties; he needed to get right to talking about the important gospel. And when he sent the letter to the slave owner Philemon to plead for Onesimus's freedom[15]—basically saying, "You owe me a favor"[16]—this wasn't like a modern-day text. Paul was spending serious money, time, and energy on the message because he believed this was a gospel issue. He was willing to risk his relationship with Philemon by speaking boldly.

The form of a first-century letter informs the way we read it and understand its intention. There is no word that is thrown in as fluff, nor is there any letter that did not have significant thought behind it. When you read the epistles, you need to recognize that every paragraph, every verse, every word holds significance. This is true of every book of the Bible, but it is especially true of the epistles, which were so costly, yet so cherished.

15. Philemon 17.
16. Philemon 19–21.

It is important to note that the epistles could be divided into those that were written to a church and those that were written to individuals, though I do not find it extremely helpful to do this because that implies they are to be exegeted[17] and applied differently. What we will find is that letters written to both churches and individuals are rather similar in application today (that is why they are canon). Both types of epistles are binding over our personal lives and the life of the church. All of the verses in them are authoritative. While some letters (such as those written to Timothy) pertain more to church leadership and organization, and therefore might feel less applicable for the average believer, they still are profitable for us to read and study because we have all been sent out to preach the gospel. Paul outlined for Timothy what it looks like to lead, preach, and minister, and we are doing similar things in our homes, Sunday school classes, workplaces, and even communities as the light of the world. Therefore, we are not exempt from the message of any letter in the New Testament. They all hold equal value and weight.

All the "Problems" in the Epistles

As we talk about the text in the epistles, it is important to acknowledge that the epistles' instructions for life and worship are some of the most debated texts among those in the church. We cannot faithfully study our hermeneutics without

---

17. Exegesis is how you interpret the Bible. Pastors do this in their sermons when they say, "This means . . ." but we also do this every day in our own Bible studies. Everyone does exegesis every time they read the Bible. Exegesis is shaped by our hermeneutic, which is what we believe about the Bible and how it is to be interpreted.

acknowledging the modern debates on gender, worship, charismatic gifts, and even modesty.

No matter what the debate is, be aware that not all debates can be settled, and that's okay. It's just fine to try to understand much of what is discussed in the epistles and the Gospels, but these things generally aren't necessary for salvation. Debates around how to do baptism aren't salvific debates. These are secondary to the gospel, not crucial to settle in order to be saved. The phrase "the perspicuity of Scripture" means that what is necessary for salvation is clear in Scripture. And here's what's clear: Jesus, who was 100 percent God and 100 percent man, died on the cross as an atonement for our sins and resurrected from the dead. What is unclear in Scripture (and therefore not necessary for salvation) are things like the specifics of baptism, women's level of leadership in the home and church, and the use of specific spiritual gifts.

Jesus tells us to follow him even when we don't have all the answers. We must hold the whole of Scripture with a holy fear and conviction. If we believe the Bible is true, we will seek to understand the debates, honor them, and not act as though we have all the answers. There are valid reasons why topics including worship, spiritual gifts, and baptism have been debated in the church for centuries. But these are conversations that need the fruits of the Spirit. If we are the people of the living God, with the Holy Spirit living inside us, we ought to epitomize the grace of Jesus Christ as we patiently wrestle with our brothers and sisters on these issues.

Remember our framework of Creation, Fall, Redemption, and Consummation? The epistles fall after the cross but before Consummation (fig. 9.1), so therefore they are the outworking of the cross in our lives, but they are not the be-all and end-all. It can be easy to forget this. We sometimes act as if someone's stance on complementarianism or baptism[18] is the most important thing. And when this happens, we focus on winning theological debates instead of winning lost souls to Christ.

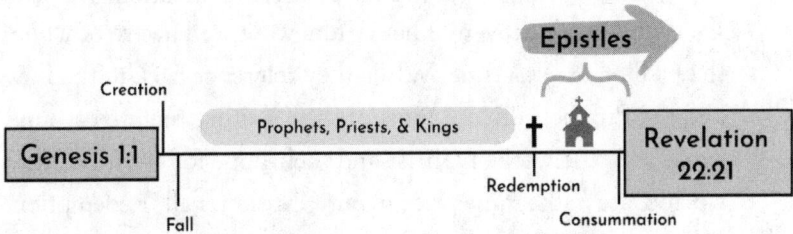

The Creation, Fall, Redemption, and Consummation framework sets us free from this mindset. We know that these epistles fall after the cross but look forward to the Consummation, heaven. When we understand this, our focus shifts from winning culture wars among the church to winning souls to Christ—because we don't have much time. We know that salvation doesn't ultimately depend on our perfect theology;[19] rather, it depends on Christ and his work (so we better get to work spreading the good news).

This also affects the way we read the epistles. We need to study them with the idea that they are pointing heavenward. You'll see how much the authors of the various epistles keep heaven as their focus in encouragement, edification, instruction, and worship. This is a huge theme in every epistle. Heaven informs the way we handle everything in our lives today—or

18. To dunk or to sprinkle? Infant baptism or "believer's" baptism? These are heated debates among believers of different denominations.

19. Though theological wrestling is important, we need to focus less on debating about them and more on studying them.

at least it ought to. For example, when it comes to the worship wars, we see that heaven has all sorts of tribes and tongues singing his praise;[20] it's not about the size of the screen, the use of a smoke machine, or the choice between modern bops and hymns.

When you're reading the epistles, notice how they work from their theology of the cross to shape the way they live to Jesus and await heaven. The writers were well aware of where they fell on the storyline. While they reference back to the Law and the Prophets often,[21] most of their writing centered around explaining the work of Christ and their hope for eternity. Since we, too, are in the same place in our Creation, Fall, Redemption, Consummation storyline, this should be our focus as well. This is also why the epistles feel so much easier to read than the Old Testament. We are at the same theological point as the epistles, unpacking Christ's death and our theology on how to live based on that (fig. 9.2). We, too, are awaiting heaven and sent out to preach the gospel to the nations. We are in the same spot in the storyline of God's redeeming his people for his glory.

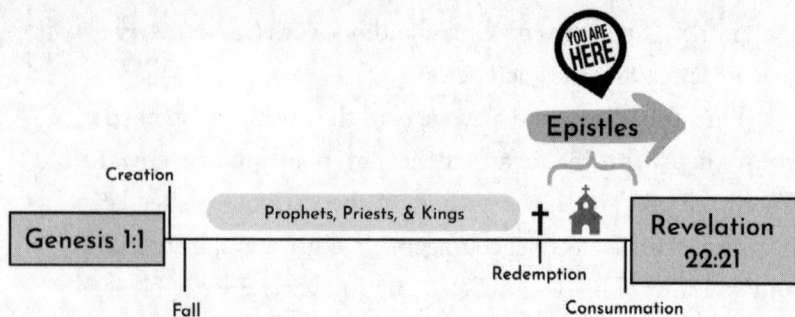

YOU ARE
HERE

Epistles

Creation

Genesis 1:1

Prophets, Priests, & Kings

† 🏛

Revelation
22:21

Redemption

Fall

Consummation

---

20. Revelation 7:9.

21. Studying the New Testament's use of the Old Testament is one of the richest studies you can do to understand the New Testament. Gregory Beale has done a great deal of work on this topic that I highly recommend.

Does this mean that we don't need to read and study the epistles? Absolutely not! They have so much to say about our lives today. Does this mean that we read only these books? Sorry, but no. I say this to encourage you that you're not crazy for feeling comfortable in the epistles. But you also need to understand that they are building off the cross, which is building off the whole Old Testament's need for a Savior because of the Fall. And it looks forward to heaven, which is the better creation—a new heaven and a new earth, where all wrongs will be made right.

As you read, keep your eyes peeled for the theological explanations of what Christ means for our lives today and the hope of heaven. Also, keep in mind these first-century Christians' cultural roots. When 2 Timothy 3:16 references "all Scripture," it is referencing the Old Testament, since Christians didn't have the canonized New Testament yet. When the early church wrestles with the new body of believers being a mix of Jews and gentiles in Acts 15, keep in mind they are interpreting the Old Testament laws and instructions for how to live and worship among those who don't follow the same cleanliness laws that the Jews did. The epistles isolated will indeed convict, but the epistles in context will change your life and the way you read the rest of the Bible.

I hope you're seeing the interrelated nature of the Bible. By the time we reach the bulk of the New Testament epistles, we aren't just looking at the life of Christ—we're also looking at the whole of Old Testament history and theology. That's why there are so many Old Testament references throughout theology passages.[22]

---

22. See, for example, Romans 5 and Hebrews 11.

This is what scholars are referring to when they use the term *biblical theology*. As those living on this side of the cross, we want to look at the Old Testament and New Testament together. We want to see how the New Testament used, referenced, and fulfilled various Old Testament passages.[23] Just as the New Testament authors were students of the Old Testament, we now get to be students of both.

Friend, do not grow discouraged, as if studenthood of the Bible is a burden. If we are going to say the Bible is authoritative over our lives, we'd better make sure we are interpreting it faithfully. It is not a burden but a blessing to have the privilege to wrestle with what Paul meant when he said that women ought to be silent.[24] That's a privilege that countless generations before us didn't have. We now have the education, resources, time, and freedom to research, wrestle with, study, and pray through these issues. Think of your ancestors. My immigrant great-grandparents left the motherland for a new life in America. Some of them were Polish women who lived lives highly influenced by religion and culture and who went to the Catholic church as Messianic Jews but would never dream of having the time and money to understand the Bible. I try to make them proud. I try to steward the blessed privilege of being able to be a student of the Bible. Whatever your backstory, you can do the same. You are more equipped than those of any generation before you to feast on the Word of God and taste and see how good he is. Clearly he's calling you to do that today. Don't miss this blessed calling and privilege.

---

23. On this topic, I again recommend Beale's work as well as Abner Chou, *The Hermeneutics of the Biblical Writers: Learning to Interpret Scripture from the Prophets and Apostles* (Grand Rapids, MI: Kregel, 2018).

24. 1 Corinthians 14:34.

Bible Nerd Notes

1. **RECAP.** Let's review the structure of most epistles' beginnings and endings.

   ○ *Greetings* tend to list the author and the recipient of the epistle. They also extend a greeting or blessing (e.g., "grace and peace") and give thanksgiving (e.g., "I thank God for you").

   ○ *Closings* tend to give a benediction, acknowledge the epistle's authorship, and send additional greetings to individuals in the receiving church.

   Consider going through a few epistles and seeing which features—of both greetings and closings—you can find. Consider copying down the structure of an epistle to tape inside the cover of your Bible, or you can make a bookmark out of it.

2. **INVESTIGATE.** I noted the interrelated nature of the epistles with the Old Testament. This can often be referred to as *intertextuality*. Read Romans 5:12–19. How does Paul build off the events of Creation and the Fall to argue for how Christ's redemption applies to us?

3. **REVIEW AND REFLECT.** I spent a large portion of this book (so far) reminding you that the Bible is the story of God redeeming his people for his glory. In this chapter we discussed how the epistles are letters written in the same "chapter" of the Bible story as we find ourselves in—after the cross, looking toward heaven. We also talked about how the epistles deal with a lot of our same questions: "How do we live today?" "What do we believe about the cross?" and "How do we worship now?" Here in the epistles it might feel the most tempting to do eisegesis. Remember, that's

when we insert our own ideas, biases, or agendas into the text (as in the example of Phil. 4:13 from chapter 1). Consider the focus of these books of the Bible and how they are not about you but are for you. These books are such gifts to believers today. May we faithfully read, respond to, and live by them.

CHAPTER 10

Not Just a Clue Book

Unless it's Christmastime, most of us avoid the Prophets like the plague. We wonder whether we ought to care about them more, but 99 percent of the church doesn't seem to enjoy spending time in Ezekiel. We read books such as Ezekiel only out of this nagging sense of "I ought to." It's sort of like the chore of cleaning out the chicken coop. Neither my husband nor I enjoy doing it. We put it off until it is well past time to do it, and then we usually just spontaneously decide "Today's the day!" And we get disgustingly dirty scraping chicken poop off the inside of the roost. We have nineteen chickens, most of which aren't of laying age yet, so cleaning the coop doesn't feel very rewarding. But we still do it. Why? Because it's necessary. If too much poop piles up in the chickens' coop, it can infect and kill them.

I bet you didn't think you'd be reading about chicken dung. But now you know that my life isn't all peachy—some days I'm covered in chicken poop and gripping tightly to the last thread of sanity I have. I also know that we all have those chores we despise. When I was growing up, it was folding socks. Today I just don't do that. They all go in their own drawer, and they are all exactly the same, so I don't have to worry about pairing socks and folding them. (I'm convinced that part of adulthood is learning how to either make the annoying parts of life easier or avoid them altogether.)

Similarly, I have grown up in multiple churches of multiple denominations, and none of them have spent any length of time studying a prophetic book. Pastors often don't have to take more than a handful of classes on the Prophets in Bible college and seminary—if any—and that kind of avoidance seeps down from seminaries into their preaching, our congregations, and our personal Bible studies. Oftentimes it feels like churches spend time in the Prophets as though it's a chore.

This, however, is when we come back to my creed: Do we really believe the Bible is true? If we do, we will read it and treat it as we should—in its entirety. We need to get dirty and messy, wrestling with what we often avoid like chicken poop or else our hermeneutic has caught the infection of neglect.

Prophecy

The prophetic books are the books that have the most interesting background history and context. Therefore, they need the most studies in context to make sure we're being faithful readers. These books preach truth against the social context of idolatry, injustice, war, famine, and other important topics, so a faithful student of the Word should first study their context if she wants to understand or enjoy the Prophets. We need to study the people these books were written for and preached to, along with when and why—and what happened after them—to understand the books' function in our canon.[1]

These books tend to be categorized into two groups: the Major Prophets and the Minor Prophets (the distinctions are based only on each book's length). But other than that they are often viewed as mysterious books that really don't apply to us anymore. In an immediate, practical sense, it may seem that they do not apply, because the majority of the Prophets tell of future events for Israel—however, there is much more to these books than just history lessons.

Most of the prophetic books in the Bible are collections of sermons and prophecies from the named prophet that were compiled from years of preaching. Trying to read these books straight through will prove incredibly challenging for this very reason. I find it most helpful to read the Prophets in chronological order along with the rest of the Bible. This means we have to take a book of prophecy in bite-size pieces, realizing that most of the time it wasn't written all at once, as an epistle was. The Prophets function as a sort of social commentary by God to his people, warning them of the consequences of their sin and idolatry and reminding them of the covenant. Therefore, their meaning is incredibly dependent on their historical situation.

These books are also highly dependent on the Law. We

---

1. When I say *canon*, I'm referring to the Scriptures—what was included and bound as the inerrant Word of God. I am a firm believer in the sovereignty (supreme power and authority) of our God and thus his sovereign reign over our canonized Bibles. I believe he really does work in, through, and despite the historical process of the church preserving, translating, and sharing the Scriptures. Therefore, as a student of the Word, I always want to ask what God is doing in the church through a particular text that I struggle to understand. I always look for how it points to Jesus, redemption, eternity, and worship.

cannot understand these texts outside of a thorough understanding of the laws and covenants of God. I wouldn't recommend a
student try to study the prophetic books before they understand
the Pentateuch.[2] We see that the Law's blessings[3] and curses[4]
have their outworking in the Prophets. There, God's people
(and their neighbors) receive the blessings of following the law
and face the curses of breaking the law. Though it is not always
fun to read about the enforcement of God's law, it does show
us God's heart for his people. Over and over again he reminds
them of his love, covenants, and provision.

We see in the Prophets how God is a passionate lover who
will shame himself to ransom his unfaithful bride (Hos. 3:1),
how he longs to dwell with and bless his people (Hag. 2:1–9),
and how he wants to fill us up to the point of overflow (Ezekiel
47). These are promises and hopes we wouldn't expect from
an angry God enacting covenant curses on his people. This is
because it isn't a different God, or a different heart, or even a different aspect of the good God in the New Testament. The more
you study the Prophets, the more you realize that his heart has
always been the same. A prophet preaching truth to a rebellious,
disobedient people is really God sending a gracious, love-filled
call to his people to come back to him. The prophets are mediators between God and humans, reminding God's people of the
covenant they agreed to.

It is also important to acknowledge that the role of a prophet
wasn't unique or culturally unexpected. There were false prophets of the day, but we see that the true prophets were the ones

---

2. The Pentateuch is the first five books of the Bible, containing texts that are
essential to our understanding of the law and the covenants.
3. See Leviticus 26:1–13; Deuteronomy 4:32–40; 28:1–14.
4. Leviticus 26:14–39; Deuteronomy 4:15–28; 28:15–68.

whom God appointed.[5] These prophets didn't speak what they hoped to be true—or even what they predicted would happen—but as mediators and messengers of God, they spoke the messages God gave them to say. This is why they consistently say, "Thus says the Lord." If something is repeated over and over again in the Bible, it's probably a theme. In the Prophets, it's not just a theme, it's their function! Therefore, it's critical for us to understand the Prophets in order to understand that they were acting as mouthpieces for God.

Different traditions and denominations still use the title "prophet" today, though it functions differently than it did in the Old Testament. The role of the prophet back then was simply to speak God's Word. The prophets in the Bible weren't speaking their opinions, hopes, or guesses—they were only speaking God's truth. Because of this, they were never wrong. They also did not tend to prophesy about individuals' lives but rather mostly prophesied over large groups of people (which would wreck our individualistic societies today). They never added to God's law, but they did clarify how Israel broke the law or kept the law, and they told of the consequences of their actions. In fact, they never shared anything new.[6] The prophets enforced the preexisting law and reminded God's people of their covenant relationship with God.

As students of the Bible, we will miss the depth in the Prophets if we don't see how heavily they are based on the law of God. And we cannot study them without also studying the law. The prophets were doing modern-day "intervention" based on

---

5. See, for example, Isaiah 6; Jeremiah 1; Ezekiel 1–3.
6. Gordon D. Fee and Douglas Stuart make this point in *How to Read the Bible for All Its Worth*, 4th ed. (Grand Rapids, MI: Zondervan, 2014), 153–55.

a set of rules or morals the people of God already knew, reminding them of the consequences they'd face if they kept walking in their ways.

I've never been a part of a serious intervention, but I can imagine the anxiety everyone involved must feel. Confronting someone who is controlled by their bad habits and poor decisions is never a fun thing to do, and we get glimpses of exactly that happening in the Prophets. But this is all part of the story of God redeeming his people. God is willing to climb every wall and break every chain to ransom us to himself.

The Bible also contains prophetic literature that hasn't been fulfilled yet, such as prophecies inside the book of Revelation. But Revelation is specifically considered apocalyptic literature.

Apocalyptic Literature

I, like many other kids who were raised in the 2000s, grew up watching the *Left Behind* movies and would frequently have moments when I'd wake up from a nap and walk around a very quiet house wondering, *Did I get left behind?*

You, too, might have fears and questions about the promised new heaven and new earth and how it will come about. Whether we're curious about the end times or experiencing the stress of an election year, the panic of a natural disaster, or the anxiety of a financial crisis, we often turn to Revelation wondering what the future holds and seeking direction and comfort. There's nothing wrong with running to Revelation for direction and comfort (that's what the book was written for), but we first need to learn a bit more about this genre.

As I mentioned earlier, Revelation is considered *apocalyptic literature*—a genre that is not unique to the book of Revelation.[7] This means there were other literary apocalypses of the first century, such as the Apocalypse of Baruch. Baruch's apocalypse also has a heavenly Jerusalem, a believers' resurrection, conflict between good and evil, and God's messages throughout. The book of Revelation and the Apocalypse of Baruch sound similar at times. Revelation is, however, the only entire apocalyptic book in our Bible, canonized as God's Word.

Different from the Prophets

Apocalyptic literature is concerned with judgment and salvation in times of trial. Unlike how the prophets communicated, apocalypses were not spoken first, then recorded.[8] These were originally written as literature. This literary genre is metaphorically rich, filled with symbolic visions of things that do not exist but represent powers, peoples, or events. Typically, the apocalyptic stories are divided into parallel cycles (which is why worldwide destruction happens multiple times in Revelation) with clear patterns[9] of events (such as judgment on the Enemy). Therefore, many are not chronological.

The Prophets and apocalyptic literature can seem like opposites: The prophets typically pronounced judgment and called on God's people to change their ways and avoid consequences, but the writers of apocalypses typically encouraged God's

---

7. See also Daniel 7–12, along with parts of Joel, Amos, and Zechariah.
8. Prophecies were also significantly shorter in length.
9. For example, John uses groups of sevens as a pattern.

people and didn't call them to action in order to change events; rather, they encouraged them to endure despite facing trials.

The purpose of Revelation is to give us the comfort that God is in control. Many readers get caught up in debates about the tribulation, the ascension, one thousand years, and other confusing topics. They tend to think it is all about the details or the order of the events and how they are all going to play out. Instead, all they really should be searching for is the knowledge that God is in control and he wins out in the end. That is all we are clearly given—and it's all we need. Whether you identify as postmillennial or premillennial, or have no idea what those labels mean, you shouldn't really be just seeking to identify with one of those groups. When we "pick" a view on Revelation, we are just picking a hermeneutic—a framework by which to understand the text and rules to follow in our exegesis. So why not slow down and look at the book a little closer, as its first audiences would have?

The early readers of Revelation would have understood that it applied to their day and age while also giving them hope for the future Consummation. Gordon D. Fee and Douglas Stuart put it well in their book *How to Read the Bible for All Its Worth*: "Most Jews in Jesus' day were eschatological in their thinking. That is, they thought they lived at the very brink of time, when God would step into history and bring an end to this age and usher in the age to come."[10] Isn't that exactly how we feel today? Remember, that's why we feel so comfortable in the New Testament books—because they are on the same "side" of the cross as we are (fig. 10.1).

---

10. Fee and Stuart, *How to Read the Bible*, 131–32.

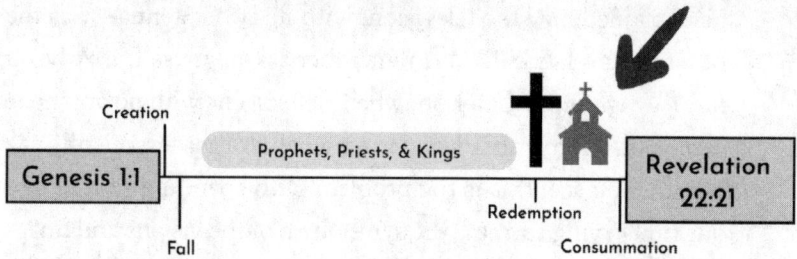

We need to remember that the function of Revelation isn't just to be relevant for our current political climate or that of AD 70. It was never really about who the twenty-four elders are, or who the second beast is, or even who the Antichrist is. If it were, John would have been clear. The whole point of a vision filled with imagery is that it is giving us a framework for understanding God's sovereignty in our trials, instead of merely telling us what to believe. But the problem is that most people want to be told what to think about each image. Even worse, there's someone out there for every view you want to find. So many prophecy "experts" are ready to call out all the other "false teachers," and it seems like each one offers his own prediction of when Jesus will come.

My father was a Hal Lindsey viewer. Lindsey was an American Christian author and evangelist known for his popular end-times prophecy books and television program.[11] I recall walking into the playroom, where our family television was, and I'd find Dad engrossed in the show *The Hal Lindsey Report*. Boy, was it a spectacle. Hal was supremely confident as

---

11. Lindsey's 1970 bestseller *The Late Great Planet Earth* popularized dispensational premillennialism, interpreting world events as signs of biblical prophecy. This book sold millions of copies and was adapted into a film. Lindsey shaped modern evangelical views strongly amid the Cold War, and his TV programs and influence spanned long after 9/11. His work remains influential in premillennial and prophecy-focused circles.

he explained how the television, with its two antennae, was the beast in Revelation 13:11. I remember asking myself, *Isn't he on the TV right now?* Later on, when flat screens with no antennae came out, I remember wondering whether those were still "the beast." You see, this is the problem with spending so much of our time trying to guess the symbolism of the visions and imagery. We totally miss the point.

Our job as readers of Revelation is to step into the various judgment scenes and images and see God victorious time and time again. God is always on the throne.[12] We are to find comfort in the promises of Revelation that Jesus alone opens the scrolls, Jesus alone has ransomed us, and Jesus alone saves. So whether this beast or that beast is ancient Rome, the former Soviet Union, or modern-day China, we know that God is sovereign over the worldly powers of our day. We ought to read and know that God alone saves. We ought to know that we, too, can lay down our crowns[13] and declare "Holy, holy, holy,"[14] because if he can conquer beasts and dragons, then no matter what persecution we face, we will always be safe in his arms.

When it comes to the meaning behind the imagery, our best option is to let the debates and theories simmer. There are times when a topic is too debated and unclear to be fruitful, but there are other times when the meaning is abundantly clear. We may not know the exact identity of the beast in Revelation 13, but we know for a fact that no matter who or what it is, God still wins out in the end (Rev. 21:4). The meaning of Revelation, while it does apply to us, is first understood through the lens of what it

---

12. Revelation 4:2–3.
13. Revelation 4:10.
14. Revelation 4:8.

meant to the early church. If we are reading about a hypothetical beast or a creature in Revelation that was an understood metaphor for Rome, it's important to know that so we stop trying to guess whether it is Donald Trump or Vladimir Putin.

I am not saying that there are no metaphors and pictures we are given to describe future events; however, I am saying that we can be so quick to try to decode the book of Revelation that we miss its historicity. After all, out of everyone who has read Revelation as a clue book and guessed the dating of the end of the world, none have been right so far. This should come as no surprise—Jesus tells us we will not know![15] If we see Revelation just as a puzzle to decipher, we are viewing it as something to be conquered, solved, or decoded. It becomes an idol of control, and our hearts begin to cry, "I must know when Jesus returns because I want to be prepared!"[16] instead of "Jesus will return—I don't know when, nor do I need to know, because I am living faithfully today."

Proper biblical exegesis should always lead us to worship. If it leads us instead to build bunkers and hoard food and guns (is my Southern showing?), we ought to reevaluate our intentions and our hearts.[17] The Bible is the story of God redeeming his people for his glory—it is all about him for us. Remember, friend, this is good news! This sets us free from the "figure it out" and "do more" mentality that so many have regarding the end of the world.

I cannot tell you how many anxious messages I have received at

---

15. Matthew 24:36.

16. In an apocalyptic text, not everything is chronological. It wasn't written to help us predict when Jesus' return will happen. That isn't the function or purpose of apocalyptic literature. Rather, it aims to give us imagery of our God conquering over evil.

17. I am not saying there is something inherently wrong with "prepping." But heavenly minded prepping is focused not on putting away food and guns but rather on sharing the gospel with the nations with a fervor because we know there isn't much time left.

2:00 a.m. from friends or family members who are stressing about the end of the world. Usually during an election season or a natural disaster, messages will pop up—especially on social media—that *this* is the end of the world. These conversations are heated—and they may even be exciting for some people—but they're filled with anxiety. That's how you know they aren't of the Lord.

When Jesus ransomed us to himself, he returned and emphasized peace,[18] so pay close attention to whoever's viewpoint on Revelation you follow, learn from, or consume. Jesus tells us in Matthew 7 that there are false teachers out there and that we will know them by their fruit. If they stir up strife and anxiety, I'd be wary of them.

Though there are many debatable interpretations of various parts of Revelation, one thing runs true through all the different understandings: Jesus wins out in the end. The main message in Revelation is this: God is in control, and he will sit on the throne, so we can trust in him.

We also need to understand that John is recording these visions with the main focus of encouraging believers who are going through tribulation. John recorded Revelation to give us assurance of who wins out in the end, not to give us anxiety about whether it's the end. I am not a fan of the mentality "Oh, well, Jesus isn't coming yet because XYZ needs to happen first." Jesus tells us to go preach the gospel and expect his return at any time. Anyone teaching "Jesus will return after XYZ" is putting the focus on things that Jesus did not. Again, this is a control-based approach to Revelation rather than a worshipful "I'm ready whenever, Lord!" that John and the apostles tend to exemplify in the

---

18. That's actually the first recorded word out of his mouth (see John 20:19).

New Testament.[19] In Acts 1:11 we read about how after the ascension their focus was on the sky—looking upward in wonder and (I can only assume) probably trying to figure it all out. But angels redirected their eyes from looking up to looking out into the world, because Jesus had just instructed them to take the gospel from Jerusalem to Judea to Samaria—and to the ends of the earth.[20]

In the same way, Jesus sent us on a mission to be his ambassadors and to preach the gospel to the ends of the earth "and then the end will come."[21] Friend, may our hermeneutic be one of worship, seeing God's mighty hand at work in both the Prophets and Revelation and responding in worship. Both of these literary genres should propel us to respond with faith and obedience. Both of these genres should encourage us to spread truth—the good news. This is the faithful reading of the Prophets and Revelation.

Bible Nerd Notes

1. **REFLECT.** I shared how the Prophets weren't adding to God's law but rather were expounding upon it. Read Hosea 6:6–7. Note how Hosea emphasizes that the law shows us our heart issues. It's not about fake obedience or checking boxes (as in "the blood of bulls and goats" in verse 6); it's about love and faith. Circle the word *love* in verse 6 where it says, "I desire love" (*love* is "mercy" in some translations). This word is *hesed*, חֶסֶד. This is a word used to describe the loving-kindness of God throughout the Bible,

---

19. See, for example, Luke 21:34–36; 2 Peter 3:10; Revelation 22:12.
20. Acts 1:8.
21. Matthew 24:14.

and God uses it to describe himself in Exodus 34:6. This means that as God has shown us love and mercy, he desires the same from us, not the lip service of checking boxes.

2. **RECAP.** Let's review some of the characteristics of apocalyptic literature:

   ○ Typically concerned with judgment on evil and salvation for believers

   ○ Written to encourage believers in times of trial

   ○ Originally written, not spoken

   ○ Lots of metaphors and symbolism—literarily rich

   ○ Often uses cycles and patterns of events happening over and over again in slightly different ways

   ○ Not chronological

   Consider writing this list of characteristics on a sticky note to place at the beginning of Revelation in your Bible, so you have a guide to aid you in your studies of this often confusing book.

3. **INVESTIGATE.** Read Revelation 6. Much debate in this chapter has been over the horsemen. Each brings destruction and judgment, similar to the four horsemen in Zechariah 6:1–8 (consider the connection they may have). After reading the chapter as a whole, ask yourself whether the horsemen are the main focus of the section. I'd argue they are not. Someone else is doing the main action of opening the seals. Who is that? *The Lamb*, Jesus. Even better, we read about all of this after chapter 4, which described God the Father sitting on the throne. So no matter who the horsemen are, God is on the throne, and Jesus is taking action. The comfort of chapter 6 is that ultimately all judgment and tribulation that may come is from God's hands. He is the one who sits on the throne.

CHAPTER 11

Not Just a Movie

I love going to the movies and becoming engrossed in a story. The whole experience is just top tier: snacks, entertainment, and no interruptions. I don't have to talk to anyone or do any chores, all I have to do is sit and enjoy the story. You'll find me with a large bucket of popcorn and thriving as I watch a romantic comedy or a historical drama, but I especially love any movie that inspires me to do big, scary things. That's what makes a movie really good, in my opinion. I love watching a character face a big obstacle and being so engrossed in the story that I forget I'm just in a chair inside a dark room surrounded by strangers.

The best part is when I leave the movies after watching a story unfold that changes my view of everything. I walk out of the dark theater back into reality and everything feels like I am looking at it in a new way. I'm no longer on the planet Endor[1] or in District 12.[2] I'm back in Dallas, Texas, and it's time to go

---

1. Thanks, *Star Wars*.
2. Thanks, *Hunger Games*.

home and get back to normal life. I'll likely get in the car and talk about the movie with my husband and think about the characters, the obstacles they faced, and how the movie made me feel.

Perhaps all too often we think of the Bible, especially the stories of Jesus in the Gospels, in this same way. But the Gospels aren't a movie with characters. They don't function simply as a story created to make you feel a certain way or inspire you to do big, scary things. The Gospels are so much more. How so?

The Gospels don't just present the cross at the end of the story as some big obstacle for Jesus to face—they portray it as the testimony of good news. The Gospels run headfirst to the cross.

A big misunderstanding around the Gospels is that they are telling a firsthand account of this great news and are written to those who already believe, reminding them of the truth they profess. And they're not just telling a story, they are testimony. They retell what we know to be true of Christ and what he did and taught because they are written to encourage the early church. The early church was made up of many believers who were under persecution. The humiliation of the cross and the suffering of Christ are huge themes of the Gospels because they are written to those facing similar suffering and humiliation. But before we can understand the theological emphasis of the Gospels, we need to first understand their genre.

The Gospels

The Gospels in the Bible are not the only gospels from the first century. *Gospels* were a popular type of literature back then.

Generally used as a means to record someone's thoughts and experiences, gospels were similar to something like the (more formal) diary or Facebook posts of the day; they looked very different depending on who authored them.

To be honest, I don't use Facebook much. (I am currently logged out and can't seem to find my way back in, but maybe the Lord is teaching me self-control against the temptations of Facebook Marketplace.) Yet what I understand about Facebook is that it can look different for everyone. Your political uncle only reposts (controversial) news commentary on his feed; your sister spends all day on the community pages for her church, neighborhood, and kids' school; and your mom only reposts your photos and her own vacation photos. If you're like me, you use it only for the great deals found on Facebook Marketplace. (I love a good virtual garage sale.)

Similarly, first-century gospels looked different from author to author. There weren't necessarily literary rules to a gospel, but they were personal accounts for whatever someone wanted to use them for. The gospels we have about Jesus that were not canonized in the Bible are those that weren't considered historical accounts but rather were categorized as lore or personal reflections. The Gospels that are canonized are historical recordings (with theological purpose and focus) of actual events and the teachings of Jesus.

While it is important to understand that gospels were a popular form of literature in their day, it's also essential to realize that the Gospels we have in the Bible are different from the other gospels of their day in that they are canonized. It is widely accepted that they were being shared and passed around in the years after Jesus' resurrection and ascension—and that these Gospels weren't like any other type of gospel. These were Gospels that God was working through. They were truth, and in them was the truth of life in Jesus. These Gospels were—and remain—God's Word.

There's really nothing in our daily lives quite like this. Maybe it's slightly similar to when a breakout song or show suddenly gains popularity because of its special take on some universal experience. We share it, sing it, and quote it because we relate to it. The Gospels we have in our Bibles today were understood to be like that. They weren't like everyone else's gospels; these Gospels were telling truth. They told firsthand accounts—testimonies of what Jesus said and did. First-century peers read them and said, "Yes! This is it. Let's share this." They told a narrative that first-century readers resonated with, experienced, and heard about from their friends and families. That's why the Gospels reference specific people, places, and events.[3] They were written in the midst of real history, and the writers wanted us to know that.

The Gospels as Theology

This leads us to the second point of the Gospels, which is that they are theological in nature. If you've ever done a close reading of any of the four gospels, you may have noticed that they do not include every date and detail like a history textbook does. They also don't contain every theological statement and meaning like a book of systematic theology would. The Gospels are the Word

---

3. See for example the reference to ancient "mutuals," Alexander and Rufus, in Mark 15:21.

of God meeting our everyday lives. So you have references to the fish the disciples ate alongside eternal truths from the mouth of the Messiah himself.

Even more interesting, these Gospels don't record *every-thing*. They record what is necessary, and they record with a theological purpose in mind. John 20:31 tells us that the gospel of John is written that we may believe. Matthew writes to the Jewish Christians to encourage them in their faith and give them confidence. Mark writes to Jews and gentiles facing persecution, highlighting how Jesus suffered so he can encourage his readers to have endurance through their own persecutions. Luke describes how Jesus came for everyone—the lowly and even the pious higher-ups.

The Gospels were written with a focus and a purpose. That's why they don't record every meal or every conversation with Jesus.[4] That wasn't the point (although that would have been cool). The point was that believers would be encouraged in their faith and come away with a stronger understanding of Jesus' message and mission—and of their call to follow him.

Right now you might be wondering what this has to do with your daily Bible studies: "Faith, what does this even mean for me and my life? What does this change?" Well, this changes everything. When you read the Gospels with this perspective, you'll know that they are not just a history or just a theology—and you won't treat them solely as either!

You'll see that Matthew included the details he included for a reason. He could have left some things out. When you come across a different order of events or details of a story in

---

4. John 21:25.

the Gospels,[5] you won't be shocked or doubt their reliability because you know they weren't written just as a history textbook—they were written with a theological emphasis. When you're tempted to skim over the genealogy presented in Matthew 1, you'll remember that Matthew was writing to a Jewish audience, and he spent time writing out that genealogy in order to emphasize that Jesus is the Messiah who had been prophesied to come from the bloodline of David.[6] Many people who make the mistake of reading the Gospels merely as a firsthand account miss the rich theological framework that shapes the way John structures his gospel or Mark ends his gospel (in a seemingly weird way[7]).

All the Gospels use their various firsthand accounts to encourage Jewish and gentile believers who were facing persecution and martyrdom, reminding them that Jesus was everything they had been looking for—and that Jesus on the cross was everything the Old Testament believers had anticipated. This is why the Gospels hightail it to the cross, because the first-century believers (and those of us today) desperately needed to see that Jesus was everything they had been looking for. They needed to receive the same message we do today: In his dying is our living. We can join with Matthew, Mark, Luke, and John and run to the cross, because this is where we are redeemed.

---

5. See the difference between Mark 14:1 and John 12:1.

6. Matthew 1:17.

7. Some manuscripts end the book with 16:8. There is much debate about whether the final verses 9–20 were original or added later due to the odd ending. Don't worry—this shouldn't challenge the reliability of Scripture, but rather if it does end at 16:8, we have this implied question: Will we follow Jesus if we are afraid? This is a large theme of the gospel written to Christians facing martyrdom.

The Gospels and CFRC

I've spoken much about Redemption. I've reiterated through this book that the Bible is the story of God redeeming his people for his glory, but remember—here in the Gospels are the pinnacle moments of that redemption being bought. The cross is the turning point in our Bibles, the place where the story goes from expecting to imparting. What do I mean by this? The *Oxford English Dictionary* gives two definitions for *imparting*: "making information known" and "bestowing a quality."[8] These are the two focuses of the New Testament following the cross.

From this point forward, the rest of the New Testament is unpacking what Jesus means for our life and worship and explaining the reality of the cross's effect on our lives. We read in Romans of soteriology,[9] in 1 Thessalonians of how to grieve, in 1 and 2 Timothy about order in worship, and in 1 Peter 2:9 that we are the chosen royal priesthood, a holy nation. Like I expressed back in chapter 4, the cross is the hinge of the Old and New Testaments (fig. 11.1). We cannot rightly understand the New or Old Testaments without the cross. So these are some of the most important pages we will ever read in our lives. These are real, historical testimonies of the life and teachings of Jesus—may we never view them as though they are merely a movie. Instead of sitting back with a bucket of popcorn in a dark room seeking entertainment, sit up, read expectantly and carefully. These are the most important writings for all human history. Do we treat them like they are?

---

8. *Oxford English Dictionary*, "imparting," www.oed.com.
9. Soteriology is our theology around salvation.

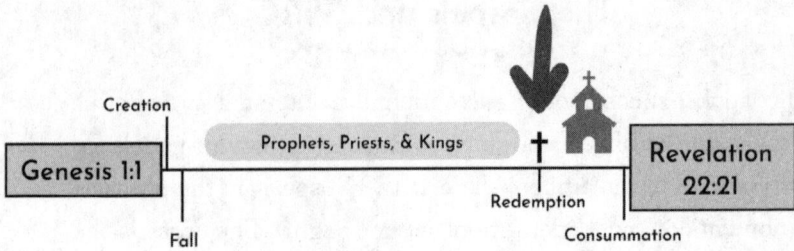

Creation — Genesis 1:1 — Prophets, Priests, & Kings — Redemption — Fall — Consummation — Revelation 22:21

Bible Nerds, may all our reading, all our worship, and all our living hinge also on the cross.

Bible Nerd Notes

1. **COMPARE.** The Gospels can be classified as testimony that is not just a history but also a theology. Because Jesus came as both God and man, he met us in our historical realities and also is God—teaching us our theology. Therefore, throughout the Gospels you see this mix of historical and theological teaching. Read the birth account from Luke 2 and compare it to the theological birth account of John 1:14.

2. **REFLECT.** How does it change your reading of the Gospels to look at them with the understanding that they are all running head-first to the cross? They don't treat the cross as some obstacle to conquer or as the climax of a great story, but as the answer to everything. They build this tension for the reader, revealing the identity and work of Jesus, and then have us stare straight into the cross and resurrection and ask ourselves the most important question of all: "Will I follow Jesus?"

3. **INVESTIGATE.** The gospel accounts have often been called propaganda. This is not in a negative sense, but they are telling

a biased testimony to convince us to follow Christ. Read John 20:31 and note John's professed reason for writing his gospel. Now read John 1:4–5; 6:33; 8:12; 10:10; 11:25; and 14:6. Notice the repeated promise in all of these and their connection to John 20:31.

CHAPTER 12

Not Just a Poem

Roses are red, violets are blue, I rarely
understand poetry, how about you?

Hi, my name is Faith, and I feel like an absolute dumbo when it comes to poetry. I loved English class growing up, except when it came to poetry. The words always seemed to melt together into one big feeling. The multiple possible meanings overwhelmed me and made me feel like it was all fluff and nothing of substance, but don't tell my high school English teacher that. She'll never forgive me.

Because of this, I avoided the Psalms for years. They overwhelmed me with their emotions, and I definitely didn't know how they were supposed to apply to my life (most the time). I'd read David's cries to the Lord and think, "Bro, same," then flip over to a book I felt more comfortable in. If you can relate to these struggles, I'm excited to tell you: I've since discovered that poetry (like the Psalms) can be information rich, theologically convicting, emotionally moving, and absolutely literarily rich. I've discovered that the Psalms are not just poems.

Years ago I decided I needed to spend more time devoted to studying the Psalms. It was due time for me to get nerdy. I started a series of in-depth studies through the Psalms where every week I'd share a verse-by-verse study with my online community. Through that process I learned so much more than I ever expected. There is not a single psalm that doesn't have rich application and conviction. Each psalm took me down a new adventure of history, theology, questions, and praise to God. The Psalms came alive to me! I pray that this chapter helps you discover the Psalms in the same way too.

The Psalter

The Psalms are partially so rich because although they feel like a ball of emotion most of the time, what they are really doing is pouring wisdom into us readers through their poetic song form. We will discuss wisdom literature in the next chapter, but all you need to know is that the Psalms are teaching God's people to remember their heritage, their identity, and their God. Contrary to my previous belief, the Psalms function not just as an emotional diary but rather as theology. It's important to acknowledge this truth at the outset because this theology also leads us to our application: Whatever truths about God that the Psalms are declaring to us are truths that the Psalms are inviting us to live by.

But one of the biggest mistakes we can make when we sit

down to read the Bible is forget that psalms were originally songs.

They are not just theological lectures or letters. They weren't written down like we have them in the Bible today. In this oral society, the people memorized musical lines by hearing and repeating them, and so the Psalms were entirely orally shared. They served as musical praises or prayers, but they weren't intended to be written down and shared in book form.

Through my close studies of the Psalms, I have learned just how integral the musical elements are to the literature itself. In their selahs (most likely musical interludes), their repetitions, and their metaphors, the Psalms give us an up-close-and-personal experience of the sung prayers and praises of God's people. These are the hummings of King David. These are the chantings of Israel on their way to Jerusalem to celebrate the Feast of Weeks. These aren't their *Time* magazine entries but rather their tear-stained, scribbled, and worn-out musical prayer journals.

The Familiarity of Broken Prayers

I've always been a prayer journaler. I've always *journaled*. There's something soothing about taking the knotted-up mess of thoughts swarming around in my head and sending me into panic and untangling it on paper. Even when I was a young girl, journaling was an outlet for me. I have boxes full of old journals, all mismatched and out of order, that hold my deepest secrets, praises, and pleas. These journals have seen me through middle school years of drama, high school years of confusion, college years of overwhelm, and motherhood years of mayhem. But I'd never tell you to go back through my old journals and do word studies on my writing, scrutinizing the metaphors or repetitions and memorizing their intricacies. I threw those pages together between fits of crying and angsty overwhelm—there's absolutely nothing thought-out there.

For years I avoided anything other than a surface reading of the Psalms. I thought that's all there really was. Surely, I couldn't actually study the words and phrases up close. It couldn't be that thoughtful! That's what I thought until I actually started to look closer. The Psalms are not like the journals we write in and never look at again—they were sung, re-sung, shared, and passed down as a core part of the heritage of the faith. In fact, they are so powerful that they were frequently quoted by Jesus! He hung on to their words and promises just as Israel did (and just as we can too). Even more interestingly, the Psalms were often not quoted exactly in the same context in the New Testament, but bits would end up pointing to Christ.[1] So the Psalms found in the Bible are different from our modern ideas of poetry, songs, or even prayers; they are unique indeed.

The Psalms are rich literary works. They frequently use metaphors and symbols to comfort and cultural references to convict or encourage singers. Psalm 40 spends the first ten verses remembering God's past mercies and then in the next seven verses pleads for God to continue to show that same mercy.

---

1. In *Modern Genre Theory: An Introduction for Biblical Studies* (Grand Rapids, MI: Zondervan Academic, 2024), Andrew Judd explains, "It is no accident that almost always when a psalm is quoted in the narrative texts of the New Testament, it is spoken aloud by a character, with the function of marking a critical moment of God's salvation and using the hermeneutical move of typology to make a Christological point" (135).

Psalm 34 uses metaphors in verses 15–16 that describe God's eyes, ears, and face to illustrate the promise that God cares about his people. Yes, David could have just said "God cares about us," but instead he illustrates it, describing God's eyes looking "toward the righteous and his ears toward their cry" (v. 15 ESV).[2]

The Five Books of the Psalter: Broken Down

The Psalms were eventually compiled and divided into five books,[3] each with its own characteristics and themes (fig. 12.1). Book one of the Psalter (Psalms 1–41) comprises mostly Davidic psalms, which means they were "written" (or sung) by *the* King David (of David and Goliath fame). These psalms tend to lean toward laments (cries of grief). Pay attention to how this book uses the covenant name of God, Yahweh (often written in all caps: LORD). It is repeated in remembrance of God's promises in the midst of these laments.

Book two (Psalms 42–72) contains fewer Davidic psalms and includes many psalms attributed to the Korahites, who were temple singers during David's and Solomon's reigns.

---

2. The Bible (and in particular the Psalms) loves to do this—restate a truth in a different way through a second, third, or even sometimes a fourth line to emphasize a truth about God. It is as if I said, "The sky is blue. Blue above my head. Bluest of blues, the airspace rules above my head." All three sentences say the same thing, reiterating the same point in a different way. This gives the singers of the psalms (or us readers) the ability to dwell on a truth. Sometimes then there is a selah to give them a musical interlude to really reflect on what they just sang. This can often be called *synonymous parallelism*.

3. Most scholars suggest this was done in the fourth or fifth century BC.

BOOK 1	BOOK 2	BOOK 3	BOOK 4	BOOK 5
PSS. 1–41	PSS. 42–72	PSS. 73–89	PSS. 90–106	PSS. 107–150

Building lament and distress

Turning Point: trust

| Lots of Davidic psalms | Psalms of Korah Psalms 42, 44-49, 84-85, 87-88 | Psalms of Asaph Psalms 73-83 | Answers the questions of book 3 | Hallel Psalms 113-18 |

| | Elohistic Psalter (uses less "YHWH" and instead "Elohim") Psalms 42-83 | | | Psalms of Ascent 120-34 |

| Lots of "LORD" (covenant name of YHWH) | | | | Lots of Davidic Psalms |

| | | Exile (no king and no temple) prayers Psalms 84-89 | "The Lord reigns" Psalms 93-100 | "Hallelujah!" Psalms 146-50 |

| Pss. 1-2 set the tone for the psalter | | | | |

Lots of lament → More praise

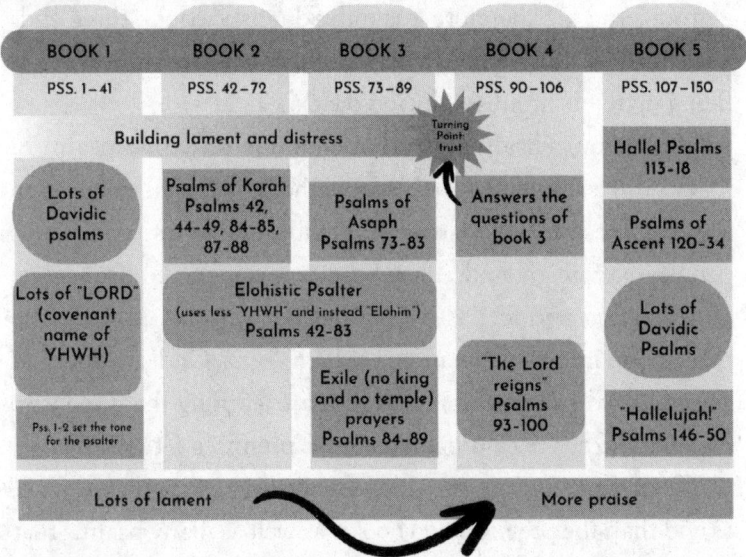

These psalms do not tend to use the name of Yahweh as much, but instead use the name Elohim (which means "mighty God" and is used throughout the Creation narrative). This change in the name of God used informs our theology because it shows that Israel is holding on to the power and all-knowingness of God (displayed in creation) in the midst of their laments.

Book three (Psalms 73–89) contains 47 percent laments,[4] which is surprisingly fewer than the previous two books. The Psalter is moving slowly from Psalm 1 to 150—from lament to praise. Book three describes the people looking to Yahweh for their joy, and many of these psalms are attributed to Asaph, who was a temple singer during David's and Solomon's reigns. These are mostly community psalms, intended to be sung as

4. Nancy L. deClaissé-Walford, Rolf A. Jacobson, and Beth LaNeel Tanner, *The Book of Psalms*, New International Commentary on the Old Testament (Grand Rapids, MI: Eerdmans, 2014), 27.

a group, and are therefore less individualistic. Book three ends with Psalms 88 and 89, two dark psalms that accuse God of not living up to his promises during the exile.

Book four (Psalms 90–106) contains only one psalm of David and is attributed to the era of the Babylonian exile, when the Israelites are really struggling with their identity as God's people in a foreign land. They have been conquered by Assyria and Babylon and feel as if God has not kept his promises to make them into a great nation (see Gen. 12:2). God's people had sinned and disobeyed him, and they are learning that God isn't the one who has been unfaithful to his promises—they are.

Book five (Psalms 107–150) contains many more psalms of David than the previous two books, as well as many psalms that served special purposes. Psalm 119 is an acrostic about the law of God that was recited at Pentecost; Psalms 113–118 are Egyptian Hallel psalms that were to be sung at Passover; and Psalms 120–134 are the Songs of Ascents, which were to be recited while traveling to Jerusalem for feasts and festivals.

As you can see, in the Psalter it is common to find patterns in the literature. One example of this is an alphabetic acrostic. This type of psalm works through the Hebrew alphabet letter by letter. Typically, each stanza will start with the next letter of the Hebrew alphabet and the psalm will focus on just one topic. The psalm will seem to repeat the same ideas, looking at the topic in a million different ways and hyperfixating on the truth it is expressing. For example, Psalm 119 is an alphabetic acrostic that praises God for his Word. Verse after verse, it uses seven Hebrew synonyms for the Torah (Law), and it is convicting, showing how much the psalmist loved God's law. It almost seems to express a ridiculous love of God's law. If you're like me, you get a couple of stanzas into the psalm and start wondering, "Is this sarcasm? How could someone love God's law *this* much?"

But what we don't see, if we're not speaking or reading in Hebrew, is that, stanza by stanza, the psalmist is working through the Hebrew alphabet! The psalmist isn't just harping on how great God's law is, he is praising God for his law, exhausting every word in his vocabulary—literally from A to Z—as a literary form of praising God with all his words! It's like a modern-day children's book: *A* is for how amazing God's Word is. *B* is for the Bible, God's Word. *C* is for Christ, the incarnate Word of God. (You get the point.) Just add in more depth and reverence, and you have something similar to the Hebrew alphabetic acrostic in Psalm 119.

Another pattern in the Psalter is the repetition of words. This is not always noticeable at first glance, because it's often synonyms or themes that are repeated, but there always seems to be theological significance to it. Through parallelism and synonyms, the Psalms are not afraid to hammer home truths using thematic repetition.[5]

Additionally, each of the first four books of the Psalter ends with a doxology in the final verses, which is a praise hymn used in worship that is sung by everyone. The final book closes with a group of psalms that function as a doxology, Psalms 146–150. Each of the first four books' doxologies is a little different, but they're all fairly similar to each other. Many scholars believe the doxologies were added after the original author's compilation of the psalms for liturgical use. The differences in endings of the five books of the Psalter are a bit like the differences in dinner-table prayers across the globe. Nearly all Christians agree we

---

5. For an easy example of repetition to spot, see Psalm 136.

should pray before a meal and bless it, but some come up with a different prayer every time, others repeat the same thing before each meal, and others sing a melodic tune. Additionally, the differences in doxologies don't call into question the reliability of the Psalms but rather enhance our understanding and application of them. For example, knowing that Psalm 41:13 is a liturgy makes me want to use it at the end of a church service or as a song.

Fairly often the Psalms offer a historical association in the subtitle such as "[Written by] David. . . . When he had fled from Saul into the cave."[6] This is a helpful tool to understand the setting, purpose, and inspiration of the song. Though scholars debate some of the historical settings, they can (at the very least) inform our understanding of how church tradition understands the historical setting. Pay close attention to who wrote the psalm, and when, and watch to see how the psalmist's theology might inform his life.

Other than the subtitles, the Psalms often refer to historical events in Israel's life such as creation,[7] the exodus,[8] the giving of the law,[9] and God's presence filling the tabernacle/temple.[10] These references to important events in Israel's history remind Israel who they are, what they believe, and what their purpose is. We, too, today, get to join with Israel and remind ourselves of our identities as God's people.

The Psalms are not mere poetry or songs, they are theological testimonies. Like the Gospels, which recorded historical accounts of the identity and teachings of Jesus, the Psalms record historical accounts of Israel's believing, doubting, struggling, and praising.

---

6. See Psalm 57 and also a similar historical reference in Psalm 142.
7. See, for example, Psalms 8, 19, and 104.
8. See, for example, Psalms 78, 105, and 136.
9. See, for example, Psalms 78, 105, and 147.
10. See, for example, Psalms 24 and 132.

We watch as Israel reminds themselves of what they believe God to be,[11] how they believe God to act,[12] and how that affects their lives.[13] As readers we get to join with Israel singing these songs and have them not just influence our worship but also become our own heart cries: in doubts, in questions, and in praise.

Bible Nerd Notes

1. **RECAP.** I gave you multiple descriptors of the five different books of the Psalms. Consider writing these attributes down in your Bible at the start of each book of the Psalms. Consider also copying the chart and placing it somewhere inside your Bible for the next time you're in the Psalms.

2. **COMPARE.** Open your Bible and compare the doxologies that end the first four books of the Psalms (Pss. 41:13; 72:19–20; 89:52; 106:48). How are they similar? How are they different?

3. **REFLECT.** Our God chose, in his sovereignty, to provide us with the Psalter, which doesn't just display perfect praise. The Psalter contains doubts and questions, and it even seems to challenge God at times (Psalms 88–89). How does this give us a bigger view of God? He's not a God who can be praised only in good times, when there are no doubts or questions. Our God is one whose reign and power are not threatened by our uncertainties or concerns. How can you bring that same kind of vulnerability into your own prayer life, to entrust everything (even disbelief) to God?

---

11. See Psalm 103.
12. See Psalm 136.
13. See Psalm 15.

CHAPTER 13

Not Just a Wise Old Saying

D o you remember where you were when one of your grand-parents passed? Chances are you're now thinking of a specific time and place, and a horrible feeling just washed over you (sorry about that). Often, losing a grandparent is the first time we experience the death of someone close to us. While I wouldn't wish grief and loss on anyone, I do think there is a God-ordained maturing that happens when we lose a grand-parent or someone close to us. We realize there's a piece of our own story in the life of the loved one who has passed. We often replay our last conversations and memories we had with them and treasure the moments we spent together all the more.

I bring this up not to make us sad but because most of us know the pain of losing someone who has poured wisdom or guidance into our lives. If it wasn't a grandparent, maybe it was a pastor who left to another church, or a close mentor who passed away. Maybe we display something, like a special picture, to remember them by, but chances are we won't think to write down their sayings. Because what they taught us is already written on our hearts.

I've had the pleasure of being named after my own role model—my mother's mother. She showed me what it is like to give at all times, not just at Christmas. She genuinely cared for the less fortunate and overlooked, and consistently put others' needs above her own. She taught me what it meant to have class, though I am still very much struggling to embody it. She also taught me the importance of faithfulness in life's storms. These life lessons didn't come wrapped in a box and tied with a perfect bow or written down in orderly fashion in a book; they were taught in the little moments of everyday life. One lesson could be taught in the Kohl's parking lot, another in a doctor's office, and yet another in her kitchen on a hot summer afternoon.

My grandmother didn't realize she was changing my life through her ordinary way of speaking and living. She was simply teaching me the way she saw the world, which she had been taught by her own mother. Her mother's mother had left everything behind in Poland to start a new life in America. Generations later, my grandmother imparted that same wisdom to me.

Similarly, wisdom literature in the Bible was treasured and passed down through the generations. That wisdom then became the identity and moral compass of many people.

Wisdom

Wisdom literature makes up a large portion of the Old Testament, yet it is not something we typically know how to read.

The books understood to be wisdom literature are Job, (parts of the) Psalms, Proverbs, Ecclesiastes, and Song of Solomon.[1] Wisdom literature in the ancient Near East was something that was memorized, repeated, quoted, and passed down, like we pass down Great-Grandma Betsy's fine china.

I don't know whether people even do *that* anymore. But when I was gifted my mother's china, and later my grandmother-in-law's, each plate was wrapped in layers of bubble wrap. Someone had even hand-stitched layers of soft fabric to lay between each of the plates. These family heirlooms had been lovingly cared for and passed down to the next generation, and their inherent value was understood and honored.

Similarly, wisdom in the ancient Near East was viewed as a valuable inheritance and asset to treasure, and therefore it was memorized, recorded, and cherished. Solomon knew to ask only for wisdom from the Lord because wisdom was what he valued.[2] Wisdom might not be something our modern-day society values, but the ancient peoples of the Old Testament understood what it was worth. Let's break down the different forms of wisdom literature in our Bibles.

Proverbs

The Proverbs are short, powerful sayings of wisdom that are all compiled into one book. Each line, or set of lines, is dedicated to a different aspect of wisdom. It would be like a group

---

1. I already included notes on the Psalms in the previous chapter, but it is important to note that there are undoubtedly themes of wisdom through many of the Psalms.
2. 1 Kings 3:1–15.

of Christians gathering together and compiling a book that read something like this:

> Be nice to your Sunday school teacher,
> He is tired and could use a coffee gift card.
> Don't yell at your kids,
> They'll remember that forever.
> Take care of your elderly family,
> Retirement homes are expensive.
> Don't shop at Nordstrom and Macy's,
> Buy used and save millions.
> When you raise your voice at your kids,
> Look them in the eye and tell them what they did wrong.

This is a short example of what we see in Proverbs. Typically, the wisdom is written in a poetic style, presented in two lines of sometimes parallel thoughts. There isn't much organization to the chapters or sections of Proverbs, and they are not authoritative for every situation in life. This doesn't mean the Bible isn't infallible and authoritative, but it does mean you need wisdom to properly apply wisdom literature to your life. For example, let's say we were trying to apply those preceding "verses" to our lives. The first verse tells us to be nice to our Sunday school teacher and gives the example of giving him a coffee gift card. But what if your Sunday school teacher doesn't drink coffee? What if your teacher isn't a man? You're not being disobedient to this verse if you give tea to Mrs. Smith, your Sunday school teacher.

You see, there is discernment that needs to be applied to the Proverbs. Additionally, there are some things that are highly cultural. For example, retirement homes for the elderly could one day become more affordable! Or maybe Nordstrom and Macy's aren't the problem—excessive shopping for luxury items is the problem being addressed. Based on this verse, some could say it is a sin to shop at Nordstrom but not a sin to shop at Prada. Obviously, neither is a sin—the idolatry of the heart is what this "proverb" is addressing. Additionally, what if you find something from Nordstrom at a thrift store? Would that make this proverb untrue or outdated? Of course not. You need wisdom to be able to understand and apply wisdom literature.

You'll also see in the Proverbs general or even hyperbolic language. What if you shop used and save only thousands, not millions? Does that make this proverb a lie? No! The Proverbs are general rules for living, but they are not promises. This means that while they provide general guidelines to live by, they don't give you guaranteed outcomes for every scenario.

You'll also notice a seeming contradiction in our modern-day proverbs. The second proverb reads, "Don't yell at your kids," but the last one reads, "When you raise your voice at your kids . . ." So what does this mean? Is it a contradiction? I would say no. But many critics of the Bible refer to examples like this in the Proverbs as contradictions. Proverbs 26:4 tells us, "Do not answer a fool according to his folly, or you yourself will be just like him," then the very next verse says, "Answer a fool according to his folly, or he will be wise in his own eyes." This seems like a clear contradiction. But these proverbs show that it is wise to not respond back to a fool like a fool but there is also a time to correct a fool. It takes wisdom to know when and how to act. Because the Proverbs speak to all of life's circumstances, they at times tell us to address the fool and at other times warn against it.

Some proverbs will, at times, seemingly contradict themselves while addressing the whole host of human experiences, but no single proverb can be taken and applied to every part of our lives. We need wisdom to know how to apply the Proverbs. Of course, everything is nuanced and everything has caveats. In fact, that is wisdom in itself: to know limits and nuance.

On that note, it is necessary to say that though the Proverbs are God's authoritative and inherent Word, they cannot always be taken literally. Proverbs 15:25 reads, "The LORD tears down the house of the proud, but he sets the widow's boundary stones in place." But this is not a promise that every proud person's house will literally be destroyed. This also does not mean that if your house is destroyed, it is because you were proud.

Here, the Proverbs are presenting the general idea that eventually God will take care of the sinful and wicked. We know that will be true in the Consummation. But it is important to see the similarity between the Proverbs and the parables of the New Testament. Jesus didn't tell parables so that everyone would understand them.[3] He also didn't mean for the parables to be taken literally. Their value was when they were not taken literally but instead understood to be symbolic of a larger truth than just a seed falling on a stone path.[4]

This doesn't mean that the book of Proverbs should be discarded and ignored. Proverbs is that much more important to seriously consider and study because it *is* so likely to be misunderstood. My earthly father has a twisted view of Scripture, yet he claims Proverbs to be his favorite book of the Bible. He loves the supposed promises: Statements such as "Do X and get Y"

---

3. Matthew 13:11–16.
4. Matthew 13:4.

feed his pride and desire to hack God. He takes verses as rules for all of life and ignores the rest of Scripture. I remember him referencing Proverbs 21:9 as his inspiration to separate from my mother. This verse reads, "It is better to live in a corner of the housetop than in a house shared with a quarrelsome wife" (ESV). But this verse is not telling believers to leave their wives the moment there is any sort of disagreement!

When we apply wisdom to our understanding of Proverbs 21:9, we can see that the heart of the proverb is for peace in the households of God's people. Instead of pursuing peace, however, my father villainized my mother as "quarrelsome" and cast her aside.

There's also nuance in the Proverbs around wealth and money. Proverbs 10:4 says, "A slack hand causes poverty, but the hand of the diligent makes rich" (ESV). This means that those who work hard will enjoy the fruits of their labor. If you are lazy, you should probably expect to live in poverty. Proverbs 21:5 says, "The plans of the diligent lead surely to abundance, but everyone who is hasty comes only to poverty" (ESV), which means the value is in the "slow grind." And Proverbs 14:23 says, "In all toil there is profit, but mere talk tends only to poverty" (ESV). Do you see the problem if someone wants to take these Scriptures literally, ignoring their intended meanings? There are so many different situations in life, and they all are to be understood from the worldview that Proverbs provides instead of taking this book of the Bible and using it as a rule book.

Finally, the Proverbs use the metaphor of two women. One is the woman of folly and the other is the woman of wisdom. Are these literal teachers? No, they are metaphorical women who represent lifestyles ruled by wisdom or foolishness, and each one calls out for people to join her side. Folly calls for the "simple" and those who "lack sense." Proverbs 9:18 tells us that those who follow her are dead and headed to Sheol. The woman of wisdom isn't just calling out. She has built her house, set her table, and sought out the simple.[5] She says, "The fear of the LORD is the beginning of wisdom, and the knowledge of the Holy One is insight."[6] She calls people not to worship themselves but to worship the Lord.

Ecclesiastes

Now let's discuss the book of Ecclesiastes. For years I completely avoided this book, forgetting at times that it was even a book of the Bible other than occasionally quoting the line "For everything there is a season." I avoided Ecclesiastes because I didn't understand it. It said things that sounded a whole lot like "Life doesn't matter" and "Give up" and "What's the point of anything?" While these platitudes matched my preteen existential dread, I was going to the Bible for encouragement. So why did this book seem to deliver the opposite?

Most of the book of Ecclesiastes is the quote of a worldly teacher. Yes, the majority of that twelve-chapter book you flip past when you're moving from the Psalms to the Prophets is a long quote—or a record of wisdom taught by essentially the secular university professor of the ancient Near East. Wisdom was valued back in that day and age. We call this "professor"

---

5. Proverbs 9:1–6.
6. Proverbs 9:10 ESV.

the Qohelet, because *qohelet* is the Hebrew word used for him, which means "preacher" or "teacher."

What is the wisdom he shares? The Qohelet, much like a modern psychology professor, goes through all the existential-dread stuff and arrives at the conclusion that all of life is meaningless. This secular teacher expresses throughout those twelve chapters that you can gain wealth but not inherit it. You can work hard and reap none of the harvest, and thus all of life is pointless. Then, in the final verses of Ecclesiastes, the writer returns as a narrator of sorts, and basically says, "Yes, all of life is meaningless if you don't fear God and obey his commands." You see, true biblical wisdom according to Ecclesiastes isn't ignoring the "wisdom" of the world but understanding what it lacks: a godly worldview. Figure 13.1 shows an excerpt of the final seven verses of the book.

Ecclesiastes 12:8–14

Even the very last words out of the Qohelet's mouth are, "Life is meaningless." This is the sum of his argument since 1:2.

8 "Meaningless! Meaningless!" says the Teacher.
   "Everything is meaningless!"
      9 Not only was the Teacher wise, but he also imparted knowledge to the people. He pondered and searched out and set in order many proverbs. 10 The Teacher searched to find just the right words, and what he wrote was upright and true.
      11 The words of the wise are like goads, their collected sayings like firmly embedded nails — given by one shepherd. 12 Be warned, my son, of anything in addition to them.
      Of making many books there is no end, and much study wearies the body.
      13 Now all has been heard;
         here is the conclusion of the matter:
         Fear God and keep his commandments,
         for this is the duty of all mankind.
      14 For God will bring every deed into judgment,
         including every hidden thing,
         whether it is good or evil.

Here in 12:9 the narrator's speech returns. We haven't heard from him since 1:1!

He says this is the conclusion we face: God gives meaning.

God's justice reigns, not our own.

God's knowledge reigns, not our own.

Interestingly, though, Ecclesiastes stands in stark contrast to the wisdom in Proverbs. While Proverbs 14:23 says that all hard work leads to profit, the Qohelet reminds us that this is not always true (Eccl. 2:18–21). Life is hard and sometimes you lose it all. While Proverbs 10:4 says (in so many words), "Just work hard and don't be lazy," Ecclesiastes adds balance to this wisdom, acknowledging that many people work hard all their lives to barely see the benefit (Eccl. 5:10–12; 6:1–2). It is easy to see that this world isn't fair and many people today work very hard without much value. These are universal wisdom anecdotes that aren't unique to just our faith—even the Qohelet could acknowledge this truth. The important thing that we get from our faith—and from the narrator recording the wisdom of the Qohelet—is that our faith defines these sobering truths. Yes, it is all meaningless and bleak—unless we have the Lord (Eccl. 12:13–14). Though we can lose it all and reap no harvest, we do have the Lord—and he is everything.

Job

This leads us to the wisdom of Job, another book of wisdom literature, which gives the point of view of someone who really does lose everything. The Qohelet from Ecclesiastes is all talk, but Job lives out this truth that everything really is meaningless without the Lord. If you are unfamiliar with Job's situation, he was a faithful man of God who had everything taken away from him. At the beginning of the narrative, we are given the point of view of someone watching heavenly deliberations between God and Satan and learning that Job will be tested. As we read, we learn that Job loses his health, his children, his wealth, and basically everything. He is left with only heartbreak and grief. His wife tells him to curse God and die, but he resists.

Any normal person reading this book should be simultaneously encouraged and challenged by Job's insanity. *Yeah, yeah, yeah,* we might think, *God is all we need, but really, Job? Are you sure you didn't do anything wrong? Are you sure you still trust God? Are you sure you didn't kind of deserve this?*

Those are exactly the questions Job's friends ask him. The majority of the book is made up of long, grueling discourses between the grieving, suffering Job and his friends, who keep stepping in to give him wisdom. If you pay close attention, most of their wisdom is "bad" or misplaced wisdom. It doesn't apply to Job's situation, and it certainly doesn't help anything. No, Job hasn't done anything wrong. No, he isn't being punished. We can relate to their "wisdom," though, can't we? These are natural human responses to suffering. The friends may have meant well, but the book of Job stands as a core part of biblical wisdom literature. Its purpose is to remind us that though you can work hard (Proverbs) and though often life just seems meaningless (Ecclesiastes), sometimes it sucks for no good reason—other than to give us yet another opportunity to be faithful to God, and that's not meaningless at all.

Sometimes God allows us to go through dark seasons. Sometimes injustice and suffering swallow us up, but God is still good. Sometimes we don't experience the joys, the harvests, or any benefit from following God, but he is still good. That's because God's goodness is not defined by our experience. His goodness isn't subject to the consequences of the Fall. His goodness is true when nothing else is. His love and kindness are real even when we can't feel them. Best of all, God never changes. So what was true about God centuries before—like what we read about in Job—is still true of God today.

Job is a pivotal piece of biblical wisdom that reminds us that even when we follow God faithfully, deeply, and passionately, we may still suffer. Suffering isn't always the result of being punished by God or not having enough faith. Suffering is simply a result of the Fall.

I like to imagine that the early church and the apostle Paul clung to Job's testimony on their most difficult days. I know I sure did when I was living with my father after my parents separated. Besides wrongly twisting biblical passages for his own use, he also put me through a fair bit of suffering as a result of his horrible decisions. Living at times without electricity and fearing that the bank would kick us out of the house he couldn't pay for, I was in constant fear. I had a box of my most precious items packed away in case the bank came to the front door and kicked us out. I wasn't sure whether that's how foreclosure worked, but my father scared me by talking about it. He viewed our situation as his own Job journey, obsessively claiming that God was testing him.

Ironically enough, all my father needed was a job. But there was a disconnect between Job's situation and my father's. Although I was young and immature in my faith, I nonetheless felt it. Job had lost everything while my father had willingly given it all up. Job had valued his children, sheep, and goats, but my father did not value his own wife or children. Job's heart was one of humility, but my father's heart was one of vindication and spiritual arrogance.

We don't choose our own Job situations and then cry out,

"Poor me! I'm being tested by God!" The whole point of Job is that he wasn't responsible for his suffering in any way, yet he still trusted God because God is good. My father took my birthday money, my Christmas money, and money strangers left in my locker (so I could buy a prom dress . . . isn't that so sweet?) and "used it on bills" because he was evil. I'm still not sure where that money really went. He was not struggling through a Job situation.

The book of Job isn't about us. Job is about God. Chances are none of us will ever go through a Job situation, because most of us will not lose it all. And when we do lose things in this life, some of those losses are a result of our sin and self-reliance. So Job isn't a book that we are supposed to necessarily read and then say, "That's what I am going through!" It's more likely to be a book that we read and say, "If Job can go through that and trust the Lord, then I can face my trials trusting the Lord too."

When we reach the end of Job, we see that the solution is to cast our eyes on God. After nearly forty long, grueling chapters of agony, as Job continues to suffer with no answer for his struggles, God steps in and puts everything into perspective. You see, the story was never about Job's suffering. The focus was never on what Job lost. The focus was always on God's steadfast love and wisdom. He speaks to Job in the whirlwind (which is a common pattern in the Bible of theophanies and prophetic encounters[7]), and, to be honest, puts Job in his place. We can almost hear the justified "sass" of God (if that doesn't sound too sacrilegious to say, but I bet there's a sinless, justified version of sass) as he speaks to Job in his suffering and asks, "Where

7. See Exodus 19:16; 40:34; Matthew 17:5; Acts 1:9.

were you when I formed the earth?" The exchange is a bit longer than that, using many metaphors from Creation to essentially ask, "Who do you think you are?" Job responds in humility: "I have said what I did not understand." Then God speaks judgment on Job's friends for "not speaking what is right." Finally, God gives Job double the blessings he had before.

The book of Job ends with all the attention on God's glory as Creator and Sustainer. God uses multiple references to Creation to teach the lesson of his control over everything. When we're reading this book, our attention should be not on our ability to control or figure out God but rather on God's sovereignty. The lesson of Job is that God is God—one who "gives and takes away."[8] God is always on the throne amid our trials. Placing our trust in him during trials is the number one thing we should do because he created and sustains all things. We will all face trials—that's undeniable (see John 16:33)—but the gift of following God is that we have the reassurance that everything is in his hands.

Song of Solomon

This next section of wisdom literature in the Bible is an area that overlaps with poetry, so keep in mind what I said back in chapter 7 about genres not being strict lines or divisions. A fairly thin line exists at times between poetry and wisdom literature in the Bible. There are wisdom Psalms that read more like long, poetic proverbs than prayers, and the poetic Song of Solomon

---

8. See Job 1:21.

is also wisdom oriented. Therefore, I group Song of Solomon into wisdom literature to simplify things. Song of Solomon is probably the book you wonder why they ever included in the Bible. A book in the Bible that celebrates sexuality in such vivid, descriptive terms is unexpected. If you're like me, you open it up and struggle to understand much of it. *Who is speaking here?* you wonder. *The woman or the man? What body part is he describing now? Am I actually allowed to read this? It's so uncomfortable!*

Song of Solomon celebrates the love between a man and a woman as God created it, and it doesn't back out of praising the intimacy of a committed relationship. One of the most helpful things to know about Song of Solomon is the phrase that is repeated throughout the book: "[Do] not stir up or awaken love until it pleases."[9] This was a verse I clung to tightly during my high school years. Most anyone can relate to the desire to feel seen and loved. We all long to be that all-important, needed person to someone else. We were created for community and relationship—that's why Adam wasn't "good" until he had Eve! (You're welcome, Adams all over the world.) Song of Solomon reminds us, though, that this kind of beautiful love cannot be manufactured. This beautiful love that God created us to enjoy is something that can't be forced or prematurely evoked without serious consequences.

Growing up, I heard about romantic heartbreak all the time. I saw firsthand the emotional distance between my mom and dad, and then I went to school and heard about my friends' breakups—all of which made me want nothing to do with love.

---

9. Song of Solomon 2:7, 3:5, and 8:4 ESV.

Why date in middle school when there's a 0.00004 percent chance you'll actually marry that person? Why date in high school when most kids don't even know who they are themselves?

I'd find myself constantly praying that I wouldn't face heartbreak. I wasn't even dating, but I was praying against the breakup—make it make sense! Eventually, after a few years of turmoil, I committed to myself and to God that I wouldn't date in high school. Once that was off the table, I could sit back and just enjoy teenage life. I didn't have to wonder whether I should respond to a text or try to figure out who my crush was because, no matter what, I wasn't going to date. I don't share this to pat myself on the back; it was incredibly easy to do because no one was really seeking to date the weird girl who couldn't even afford a prom dress. But I share this because the wisdom of Song of Solomon was what I clung to when I felt lonely and unwanted. Those are the aches of the heart that pierce deep. "Do not stir up or awaken love until it pleases" really hits when all you want to do is feel as happy as everyone around you seems in their relationships.

Song of Solomon is strikingly similar to the Egyptian love songs of the day. The book is written in the literary form of a celebration of love that these ancient Near Eastern people knew. God wrote it in their context, in the way in which they saw in the world. It's similar to how the pop Christian songs on the radio often (or at least used to) copy the mainstream music of the day. Song of Solomon is a contextualized love song that is patterned after the secular love songs of that day and age. But does this mean that it isn't useful or edifying for us today in our spiritual walks with the Lord? Absolutely not!

Song of Solomon hits even deeper than a love song. It isn't

just wisdom about love and romance, there is rich theological conviction woven throughout the book, which does exactly what high-school me needed: It applies the theme of passionate love in a relationship to our relationship with the Lord. There is another word repeated throughout the book, which is "Beloved" (דּוֹד; *dowd*). This word could also be translated as "loved one." Amid a framework of two people in love, we see language used over and over that they are each other's "beloved." Then the women of Jerusalem pipe up and sing about the love, and we are continually called to not stir up or awaken love until it pleases. Do you see what Song of Solomon is teaching us here? It's showing us the example of a committed, covenantal love. This isn't a crush. This isn't lust. This isn't desperation for a date to go to prom with. This is so much deeper. This is committed love.

The passion between the two lovers reflects God's passionate love for us, his people. As the groom sings to his beloved bride, we are compelled to think about the love of Israel's beloved: Yahweh. The groom has exclusive love for his bride, and the reverse is true: Israel is called to reflect that same exclusive love for Yahweh. In a time when Baal and Asherah were so tempting, promising worldly comforts and societal acceptance, Israel is called to have eyes for Yahweh alone.

Can't we all relate to this in a very real sense? Maybe you didn't take a vow to not date in high school (maybe you wish you had, or maybe you're grateful you didn't), but maybe you, too, have been through lonely times when you've desperately longed to be seen, desired, and chosen. While the world looked happy in their relationships, you were called, like Israel, to have eyes for the Lord alone. You were called to not stir up or awaken love until it pleases. While the Elvis Presleys and Taylor Swifts of the world may sing of their loves and breakups, we sing of the love of the Lord, which is unfading, never going to end in a breakup, and always for us. Praise the Lord for that!

Similar to how Ecclesiastes and Job both end, Song of Solomon ties everything together at the end. A characteristic of wisdom literature is exhausting a topic, then reaching the end and coming to a theological conclusion. Song of Solomon does this by declaring that this kind of beautiful love comes only through pure commitment and intimacy (8:6). This verse is a turning point in the book, which sets our eyes on Christ for those of us reading now after the cross. This verse reads:

> Place me like a seal over your heart,
>> like a seal on your arm;
> for love is as strong as death,
>> its jealousy unyielding as the grave.
> It burns like blazing fire,
>> like a mighty flame.

The love sung of here is a love that took Christ to the cross and overcame the grave. This is the love God held for his people throughout both the Old and New Testaments. That's why it uses metaphors like *seal* and *fire*, and later *water*, which are used elsewhere in the Bible as metaphors to describe God's love for Israel.[10] Song of Solomon wasn't just written to make us blush. It wasn't written to make us realize just how lonely we are. Song of Solomon was written to show us, through a real example of the relationship of two lovers, that God's love is committed,

---

10. For *seal*, see Jeremiah 32:10–15, 44; Haggai 2:23. For *fire*, see Malachi 3:2–3; Zechariah 13:9; Ezekiel 22:17–22. For *water*, see Ezekiel 47; Isaiah 35:6–7.

steadfast, and sure. God uses an example we all long for, a heart cry everyone has, to say, "I'll fill that."

Through these mini studies on the various genres in Scripture, I pray you see how form doesn't always necessitate function, but the form of the text informs our understanding of the intentions behind who wrote it and why it was written. Those are the questions we have to ask ourselves as we read the Bible, or we are likely to read our own context, problems, and questions into the text and misread the intended message. If we believe the Bible is true, however, we will not knowingly misuse it but rather passionately pursue the most faithful exegesis and use of the text because it *is* truth. There are many places in Scripture where things are gray and disagreements ensue (the subject of baptism, for example), but the aim isn't to always figure out the perfect answer but rather to do our reasonable best to be faithful to context, genre, the author's intention, and the unity of Scripture.

A good example of this is the use of the Old Testament in the New Testament. There are times when our genre studies will fail us and something taken from the Prophets or Psalms appears to be used completely out of context by Jesus or the author of the book.[11] But proper hermeneutics and exegesis look at not just genre, intention, and context but also how the rest of the Bible uses or references the portion of Scripture we are looking at. This is called *intertextuality*. The texts in the Bible build off and reference each other.[12] Additionally, we are looking

---

11. For example, see how Matthew 2:15 uses Hosea 11:1. For guidance on why that is *not* a misuse of Hosea 11:1, check out Abner Chou, *The Hermeneutics of the Biblical Writers: Learning to Interpret Scripture from the Prophets and Apostles* (Grand Rapids, MI: Kregel, 2018).

12. For more on intertextuality in Scripture, see Chou, *Hermeneutics of the Biblical Writers.*

at Scripture that is literary in nature, using metaphors and genre, but is also holy (this is important and basically *why* we're even reading it in the first place). It is going to stick to the literary "rules" of genre, metaphor, and so on, but it will also break those rules at times because it is the holy Word of God, revealing spiritual and not just material truths.[13]

This is why it is so important for us, as students of the Word, to look at Scripture from every angle it gives us and evaluate ourselves (and our hermeneutic), asking whether we are being as faithful to the meaning as possible. This should feel not like a burden but rather like a blessed privilege that we get to pursue a faithful reading of the Bible. We are some of the very first generations to have access to so many translations and scholarly resources. Feast on the Word. Taste and receive the wisdom in the Word, and never lose the fire he has given you for it.

Bible Nerd Notes

1. **RECAP.** Remember to use wisdom when reading wisdom literature in the Bible. The wisdom shared in the Bible can come in the form of songs, short sayings, poetry, and even narratives, and it is different from straightforward laws or simplistic stories. The goal of wisdom literature is to shape the way we view the world and respond to brokenness and sin, not to create dogmatic rules about every situation in life. While it might not always tell us exactly where to live or work, it gives wisdom to live by.

---

13. It is also important to note that first-century Jewish hermeneutics were different from ours today, but that does not give us a license to misuse the Word.

This wisdom then shapes the way we approach life's decisions. More important, wisdom literature always points to how God and his ways are greater than the world.

2. **INVESTIGATE.** Read Ecclesiastes 3:16 and compare it to the constant call throughout the book of Job for God's justice (8:3; 27:2; 31:6; 36:6; 40:8). Does Ecclesiastes really mean to tell us that there never is righteous justice? Now read Psalm 89:14. This verse tells us that God is always just. Job professes that truth even through unfair trials, and Ecclesiastes shows us there is no justice without God.

3. **REFLECT.** Notice how biblical wisdom does not ignore real life (the world or suffering). True wisdom empowered Job through the worst of the worst. True wisdom puts the teaching of the Qohelet in its place. True wisdom doesn't fear the sufferings, lies, or influences of the world because true wisdom has a very high view of God (see Job 38–42). A high view of God is seeing him as one who is big enough to work in, through, and despite our sorrows, the world's issues, and even our own fears. What a glorious joy it is that God doesn't rebuke those things but meets them with his fullness! In what ways can this change the way you struggle through hardships?

CHAPTER 14

Problems in Modern Interpretation and Application

Growing up, I had a fairly problematic speech impediment. I started sucking my left thumb when I was still in the womb, continuing to do so until I was ten years old. When I was born, my mouth was shaped to my thumb and the inverse was technically true too. If you've watched any of my YouTube video tutorials, you will notice I have what is referred to as a clubbed thumb on my left hand. Although I am fairly insecure about it, I've never lost a thumb-wrestling match with my left thumb, so she's a winner. (Plus, one of the most beautiful women in Hollywood, Megan Fox, has two of these ugly clubbed thumbs, so I like to joke I'm only half as ugly as she is.)

Nonetheless, I grew up with a speech impediment because of this thumb-sucking habit, and it still sometimes slips through when I get excited and talk fast. I remember I didn't realize it was a problem until one day at school when a boy stole my pencil. It was my favorite pencil and he would not give it back. (Yes, even back then I was a stationery nerd!) I still remember his smirk as I asked him to please give it back and he refused. So I marched my little bottom up to the teacher's desk and tried to explain the problem. But because my *R*'s were nonexistent and my consonants were all blended together, the teacher could not understand what I was so passionately trying to tell her. I'll never forget the feeling I had as second-grade me stood there at my teacher's desk just trying to get my pencil back while my teacher stared at me with a blank look on her face. Shortly after, I started attending speech classes, where I learned to slow down and pay closer attention to the sounds and shapes my mouth made and did exercises where I imitated how adults made those sounds. The first step in growing out of my speech impediment was the awareness that important people like my teacher could not understand me!

We need to step back and become aware of our approach to the Bible, much like I needed to become aware of the sounds coming out of my mouth. We also need to listen to teachers and see how they treat the Bible,[1] like I needed to step back and listen to how adults pronounced words. If we can slow down like second-grade Faith did and pay closer attention to our hermeneutic (how we read and interpret the Bible), we will find that God speaks through all texts in the Bible.

---

1. Consider E. Randolph Richards and Brandon J. O'Brien, *Misreading Scripture with Western Eyes: Removing Cultural Blinders to Better Understand the Bible* (Downers Grove, IL: InterVarsity Press, 2012). This book does a great job of closing the gap between the cultural dynamics of the biblical world and our twenty-first-century understandings. There is much that we miss when we do not consider our own misinterpretations, like my second-grade mispronunciations. Poor girl.

As you recall, the Bible is the story of God redeeming his people for his glory. The biggest beginner mistake I see Christians make when they read the Bible is that they read it looking for themselves. They look for God to part the clouds and speak to them about their immediate problems: "What car should I buy?" "Whom should I marry?" "What job should I take?" By doing this, however, they rob themselves of the depths of the Word of God and miss that God is speaking to *all* of us— and in a much more encouraging way than just telling us what specific personal choices we should make.

If you approach the Bible asking, "Where should I go to college? God, should I go to Texas A&M or Baylor?" and if you happen to flip open to Hosea 13:8 and read, "I will fall upon them like a bear robbed of her cubs; I will tear open their breast, and there I will devour them like a lion" (ESV), you might think, *Oh! God said "bear," so I should be a Baylor Bear!* Or you might read that verse and understand the bear is a beast that is destroying someone and think, *God is telling me Baylor Bears will destroy me—and therefore I must be called* not *to go to Baylor. Texas A&M it is, then!* It is all based on *your* judgment and *your* understanding and not on what the text originally meant—or means today. While it does take more work to understand Hosea and some context about that book, I hope you have already begun to find helpful guidelines in this book to support you in your Bible reading so you understand some context, no matter what book you are in. For example, from what we already learned, Hosea is a prophetic book and therefore points forward to our perfect prophet, priest, and king—Jesus. Also, we know that as a prophetic book, Hosea is reminding God's people of the law and pointing their hearts back to him. Rightly understood, this verse could never be about Baylor or Texas A&M, but it has always been about loving God first, above anything else.

When we approach the text looking for ourselves and solutions to our own problems, we miss that Hosea is a prophetic book that was written to call the Northern Kingdom of Israel to repentance and obedience after their disobedience and to warn them of the coming Assyrian invasion if they didn't repent and obey. The prophet Hosea is called to marry an unfaithful woman as a symbol of God's love and commitment to us despite Israel's unfaithfulness. Additionally, Hosea is a book full of metaphors, such as this bear in 13:8 that speaks of God as a strong beast fighting for our attention and love. It wasn't written to help ancient Near Eastern people decide what overpriced college to go to; it was written to show us God's unfailing love despite our unfaithfulness. And it was written to call God's people back to proper worship and obedience.

We must understand the context of Hosea (why it was written, to whom it was written, and what its point or focus is) in order to understand the application (fig. 14.1). You can't get to application for your life or the church's life at large until you understand the original application, purpose, situation, and so on.[2] When you understand this passage of Hosea in that way, you see that this section of the book is centered on the judgment of sin. God's people are being forewarned, reminded, and redirected because of their idol worship. God is fighting for their obedience because he is a just God who will take vengeance on evil. To describe his righteous fury against evil, he uses the similes "like a lion," "like a leopard," and "like a bear."

---

2. Unless you're wanting to misuse it. But those who willingly misuse the Bible are those who do not really believe it is true.

Hosea 13

Context starts first with the title of the chapter, informing us of the main idea. This is not a section about college or even about choosing a college to attend!

The LORD's Anger Against Israel

13 When Ephraim spoke, people trembled;[1]
    he was exalted in Israel.
But he became guilty of Baal worship and
    died.
²Now they sin more and more;
    they make idols for themselves from
        their silver,
cleverly fashioned images,
    all of them the work of craftsmen.
It is said of these people,
    "They offer human sacrifices!
    They kiss calf-idols."

Describing idol worship

³Therefore they will be like the morning
    mist,
    like the early dew that disappears,
    like chaff swirling from a threshing
        floor,
    like smoke escaping through a
        window.

THEY WON'T LAST

Remembering the exodus (and other past provision) should lead us to greater faith and not idolatry.

⁴"But I have been the LORD your God
    ever since you came out of Egypt.
You shall acknowledge no God but me,
    no Savior except me.
⁵I cared for you in the wilderness,
    in the land of burning heat.
⁶When I fed them, they were satisfied;
    when they were satisfied, they
        became proud;
    then they forgot me.
⁷So I will be like a lion to them,
    like a leopard I will lurk by the path.
⁸Like a bear robbed of her cubs,
    I will attack them and rip them
        open;
like a lion I will devour them —
    a wild animal will tear them apart.

our verse today!

⁹"You are destroyed, Israel,
    because you are against me, against
        your helper.

¹⁰Where is your king, that he may save
        you?
    Where are your rulers in all your
        towns,
    of whom you said,
        'Give me a king and princes'?
¹¹So in my anger I gave you a king,
    and in my wrath I took him away.
¹²The guilt of Ephraim is stored up,
    his sins are kept on record.
¹³Pains as of a woman in childbirth
        come to him,
    but he is a child without wisdom;
    when the time arrives,
    he doesn't have the sense to come out
        of the womb.

Another metaphor like the bear in v. 8

¹⁴"I will deliver this people from the power
        of the grave;
    I will redeem them from death.
Where, O death, are your plagues?
    Where, O grave, is your destruction?
"I will have no compassion,
¹⁵   even though he thrives among his
        brothers.
An east wind from the LORD will come,
    blowing in from the desert;
his spring will fail
    and his well dry up.
His storehouse will be plundered
    of all its treasures.
¹⁶The people of Samaria must bear their
        guilt,
    because they have rebelled against
        their God.
They will fall by the sword;
    their little ones will be dashed to the
        ground,
    their pregnant women ripped open."

Looking at a larger section, and not just a single random verse, gives a bigger more in-depth look.

Even more notable, the people of Israel would have immediately recognized these as animals of attack, not zoo animals, as we might think of them. As the verse goes on, the animals move from lurking and falling upon them to tearing them open and devouring them. This description should send chills down our spines! It is a warning against the deceit of sin and a reminder of God's vengeance against evil.

Now that we understand a little more about context (though we could spend many, many more pages on it), we can see that Hosea 13:8 isn't as simple as just a verse about college mascots. It is a verse that stands as a testimony of the ferocious love and jealously God has for our hearts, and it tells us that we should not run after idols. From there we can explore the application to our hearts and lives today. Maybe it convicts you of some idolatry in your life or encourages you in God's powerful love and pursuit of you. The Bible reframes our everything. It resets our worldview and speaks truth into our broken lives. Oftentimes when I go to Scripture, my problems seem to fade away because I realize they really aren't as important as I'd thought they were.

The Solution to Our Self-Centered Hermeneutic

When we read the Bible, we should not read it with the goal of just walking away with our own personal application. If that's the case, then we have a self-centered hermeneutic. Rather, there should be a global, church-wide application along with every personal application. If the takeaway is one that cannot be preached next Sunday in your church *and* in New City

Fellowship in Nairobi, Kenya, then it is likely too limited of an application. Even worse, you are probably missing some of the richness of the text. Don't confuse what I am saying to mean that no super-personal, convicting application ever comes from reading the Bible. I am saying, however, that for every personal application there is a larger application that anyone in the world should get from the text as well. If you miss that global application, you are missing some of the depth.

Let's use Hosea 13:7–8 as an example. While you were praying about what college to attend, you happened to flip open your Bible to Hosea 13, where you saw the odd verse about the bear. Hopefully, you now understand why it would be problematic to just say, "Oh, there's a bear in the verse! This means I should go to Baylor!" Instead, you should see the need to understand the context of God's judgment on sin and his furious jealousy for our hearts. Instead of giving you an answer to a specific question, God is calling you to sit in faith that he will guide you.

But the application doesn't end here—it is also important to note what applies to everyone through all seasons of life: God wants our hearts. He wants our worship, and he is jealous for our passion. God will not stand by and watch us fall into sin and idolatry with his arms thrown up as he sighs, "What a bummer! Another one bites the dust!" He will fight for us, tearing us open to our hearts. God is the romantic fighter, battling for our hearts' worship, love, and adoration. *That's* what this verse means. Friend, that is a better comfort than if God were to spell out in the clouds what college to choose or what person to marry. We aren't ever really seeking for the answer we think we are when we come to the Bible asking "What college should I go to?" or "Should I take that job?" No, what we are really seeking, if we are honest with ourselves, is assurance that God is in control. He loves us and is guiding us. He really does have us!

Understanding this application means even if the next time you read this verse is seventeen years later, the rich application still stands. God has you. God loves you. He is in control. This is the true application that leads us not to further self-centered thinking and self-worship but to God worship. When we turn to Scripture and are reminded that God is like that bear fighting for our hearts and our attention, that he is King of the earth, and that he loves us so passionately, we are reminded that the big, grandiose story doesn't begin or end with us. We are set free from self-focused hermeneutics and exegesis into God-focused application (worship).

Since the Bible is the story of God redeeming his people for his glory, it is his story (yes, I am aware we already addressed this, but stick with me for a second). If it is God's story revealing his love and glory—the Old Testament pointing to Christ and the New Testament revealing Christ—then no matter where you are in the Bible, all of it will reveal the truth of his power, love, glory, and will. So no matter what part of Scripture you're reading, application should always lead you to worship.

Friend, this is good news! It should feel not like a slap on the wrist but instead like a big sigh of relief. God isn't asking you to read through a bunch of confusing clues or add this random number to that random number to decode the answer to your problems. He declares repeatedly throughout Scripture that having the right understanding of who he is will solve your problems and answer your questions. Right understanding (that leads to worship) is the right application.

Because what if—and this might be getting a little edgy here, but stay with me for a second—what if God isn't waiting for you to figure out the clues as to what to do with your life but is instead working in, through, and despite the decisions you make? I am not saying our decisions—even our microdecisions—aren't important. I am also not saying that we don't have a free will, which does have consequences. What I am saying is that we have no reason to believe that God can't work in, through, and despite our missteps. He didn't wait for Moses to decode some hint before parting the waters through him. He asked for Moses to wholly trust him and worked through that faith. He never waited for Joseph to figure out exactly what the dreams meant so that he could save him; no, he was working to save him in, through, and despite Joseph's dream interpretation. Even through the cupbearer who forgot the dream interpretation![3] It is always, always about the heart. It is never just about the actions, but actions do follow the heart's posture.[4] Our actions and obedience should be road signs along the way that reveal what we worship. Our priorities reveal our idols. Our distractions reveal our doubts. Our goals reveal our worship. Our neglect reveals our disbelief.

The Familiarity Poison

If you're like me and have spent a lot of time in Christian circles, you're familiar with many passages of Scripture. It's

---

3. Genesis 40:23.
4. This refers to a person's spiritual disposition toward God, others, or a situation. It reflects a person's humility, faith, sincerity, or openness to truth.

rare for me to be hit deeply by a Bible verse that I've never heard before. Scripture starts to feel like those worn-down Walmart-brand shoes I bought last summer. This is what I call the "familiarity poison." It seeps in slowly, sprinkled with pride, whispering, "You already know this!" Sometimes it comes on like a little spark when I hear my pastor speak. "Oh! Yeah, this is *that* verse." Friend, that is the familiarity poison. Because, no, you don't know that verse. You might have heard it before. Maybe you even did a whole week of vacation Bible school based on that verse, but you likely don't know the depths of it. The moment you tell yourself you know that verse, you assume you know all the context, meaning, and application. But then, if you aren't willing to learn more about it, how will you ever grow?

The familiarity poison always feels good as it goes down. We drink it up, believing we know so much. We sit up a little taller, feeling as though we "belong here" because the pastor is preaching on our favorite verse.[5] Hear me when I say this: It is not a sin to really know a verse of the Bible or to feel like you're familiar with it, but be careful that you don't get too comfortable with this state of familiarity.

For example, the Noah narrative is classically popular. Take a moment to think about what that story teaches us.

Maybe you thought of a lesson around "faithfulness" because Noah had to trust God and be faithful to build the

---

5. Some even call these "life verses." That's a dangerous heart state to peg something as your life verse, as if you know everything there is to know about it or live unto only one line of Scripture. Be careful about assuming you have any passage of Scripture mastered or claimed. This gives a false sense of putting God in a box, compartmentalizing the truths of Scripture, instead of letting Scripture rip us open, expose our vulnerabilities, and wreck our world.

boat like God instructed him to do. Maybe you thought of a lesson around "doubt" because Noah famously didn't doubt God. But I'm guessing you probably didn't think about a lesson around "drunkenness," because it's not so well known that Noah immediately got drunk and sinned right after getting off the boat.[6]

It's so much more than just a lesson about faithfulness, because Noah's deliverance on the ark points to the deliverance that Christ provided to us. He delivers us from the waters of sin we're drowning in, and just as Noah trusted God and got in the boat, we, too, can trust in Christ's sacrifice on the cross. Instead of a boat, it is Christ's flesh and blood that we ride on. (When we take Communion, it is a symbol of our trust in Christ's payment. I like to picture it like God's arms wrapping tight around me, pulling me close in love as he rescues me from the tumultuous waters.)

The familiarity poison ruins our hermeneutic and exegesis because it tells us we already know what to expect from a passage. We open up the Bible to Proverbs 31 expecting it to convict us in our motherhood or wifehood, forgetting that it should also convict us in our worship, tithe, and rest. Just because we read that one book about Proverbs 31 that told us to try harder and be a better wife, our hermeneutic is now defined by that framework. Friend, do your best (though at times it will feel nearly impossible) to strip yourself of these presumptuous views of the text and instead look at it with fresh eyes. You just might find new things, with greater conviction, encouragement, and application than you ever expected.

---

6. Genesis 9:21.

Beware the Student's Paralysis

Perhaps you're feeling drained by all of this talk about how to read the Bible, and it's starting to seem like you'll never feel comfortable in God's Word. Perhaps you're thinking I'm making this too complicated: "Faith, isn't this too much studying about how to read the Bible instead of just reading the Bible? Isn't it sort of a lost cause?" Friend, while I did just make your view of the Bible entirely more complicated, knowledge is a blessing to steward.

No matter how long you have been a Christian or how long you have studied a passage of God's Word, the good news is that there will always be more to learn. No one will die having conquered the Bible—or even a book of the Bible. We are standing on thousands of years of work by Bible scholars and theologians, with more resources than ever, yet we will never exhaust the depths of the glory of God in his Word.

Praise the Lord! This is good news, reminding us that it's not about accomplishing something or conquering a book of the Bible. Rather, the Lord has invited you on this lifelong journey exploring the depths of the richness of Scripture. The Enemy will tell you it's about accomplishing some task—reading the whole Bible, filling your Bible with notes, finishing a book of the Bible. But true studenthood (like what we talked about in chapter 6) isn't ever accomplished or finished, it is just worship. So don't let the Enemy paralyze you in fear that you'll read something wrong, learn under a bad teacher, or something else. This isn't a performance, it is just worship. After all, making it a performance would be making it about us. And this is the story of God redeeming his people for his glory. So join in with every page, paragraph, line, and word of Scripture in the praise of our good God—he gets all the glory.

Bible Nerd Notes

1. **RECAP.** The next time you sit down to study your Bible, use the following questions as a guide to take you deeper into God's Word. Consider writing them down in the front cover of your Bible, on a bookmark, or somewhere else where you'll be reminded to use them the next time you feel overwhelmed or lost in a text.

   - Where does this book fall on the Creation, Fall, Redemption, Consummation storyline?
   - Who wrote this and to whom? Why?
   - What is the point of the book and chapter?
   - Where is Jesus in the text? How does this passage apply to believers today?
   - What do I not completely understand about this passage?

2. **USE.** If you have a hard time answering any of these questions about the meaning and historical background of the Bible's books, consider purchasing a resource that simplifies this work for you. Works such as Gordon D. Fee and Douglas Stuart's *How to Read the Bible Book by Book: A Guided Tour* do a good job of summarizing the historical background information for every book of the Bible. Also consider purchasing a study Bible that provides this background information at the beginning of every book. There are many to choose from.

3. **REFLECT.** When it comes to our application of the biblical text, I encourage you to step away from a fear-ridden, solutions-based hermeneutic. God isn't waiting for you to figure out the clues as

---

No More Boring Bible Study

to what to do in your life—he's big enough to work in, through, and despite the decisions you make. How might this set you free from a fear-ridden reading of the text to a more worshipful study of the God revealed in our Bibles? Does anything come to mind that you possibly may need to trust God more with? He is worthy of that trust.

CHAPTER 15

Digging Deeper into the Word

N ow that I've thrown all of this information about the Bible at you, you might have already begun applying it in your Bible studies. Or, if you're anything like me, you might really be "in your head" about it, unsure of what it all means. This chapter breaks down the different ways I apply the knowledge we've discussed about Bible study, to go deeper into study and reveal the richness of Scripture.

I love to say, "The Bible doesn't have to be boring!" That's because the Bible *isn't* boring. The Bible is a dynamic book. It is also the authoritative Word of God. It should hold dominance in our lives and speak into every aspect of our living out our faith. Because it is the true, living, authoritative Word of God, we should be faithful to exactly what it says for our lives today.

You might be wondering how you can find out what the context of a certain passage is. Or you might be wondering how you can learn about ancient Near Eastern history, culture, and beliefs so that you can be as faithful to the text as possible. The answers to these questions aren't secrets; rather, they are tools that many people don't practice using enough. I'll be honest with you—in my experience, getting both an undergraduate and a master's degree in biblical and theological studies, professors don't typically train pastors and teachers how to use these tools. It's through years of practicing using them that you learn when to use what tool and where to use it.

I imagine this is how woodworkers feel when they are building something. I have always wanted to grow in my woodworking skills, but I end up cutting corners (not literally) and not planning out my projects well enough. I always seem to run out of wood, measuring once and cutting fifteen times, and my projects never seem to turn out quite right. Experienced woodworkers, however, know exactly how to plan and what materials to buy, not because they're smarter than the rest of us, but because they've done it so many times. They know the right grit of sandpaper to use. They know what tools they'll need because they have done this before.

Similarly, these tools I will walk us through are ones we must put time and practice into in order to become more comfortable using them. If there was ever a time when it was important to put extra energy into practicing doing something right, it is now.

Plus, information is tricky. Can we just be honest? I will always feel a little bit of impostor syndrome when I read the works of brilliant biblical scholars. I will always feel a little like a poseur who is trying to glean something from the scraps or crumbs of wisdom these incredibly smart people may drop.

I know it can be confusing at times when you begin your morning Bible study and your brain is operating at only 45 percent because the coffee hasn't kicked in yet. You find yourself in Haggai trying to remember the book's situation, time, and audience and how it relates to your mom life of dirty diapers and spit-up. Or maybe you sit down with your Bible at lunch break during your nine to five, and you're feeling exhausted, empty, and discouraged—right now you just need a pep talk from Jesus, not a history lesson.

If you've grown up in Christian circles that treat Jesus like a commodity to consume and spit out before you move back into normal life, it can seem daunting to slow down and ask questions such as "Who was the original author and what did he mean?" But again, if we believe the Bible is true, we will want to be faithful to it and not misuse it.

Every day I write my sons love notes and hide them in their lunch boxes. My youngest son can't read yet, so his notes usually have a lot of hearts and smiley faces and drawings of us as stick figures holding hands. Despite the fact that these are fairly pitiful excuses for love notes, I want my boys to be reminded that they are my beloved sons.

This is no original idea—my mom did this for me. I can still picture the pink Crayola ink on the folded paper towels, the smiley faces, and her handwriting. I remember opening up my lunch box in the cafeteria at school and the feelings that washed over me when I pulled out one of her notes—feelings of embarrassment, sure, but also pride that I was loved. I didn't want anyone else to see how much these messages meant to me, but I was also happy that my mom loved me enough to write these notes. So now I continue this tradition with my own kids. It's a sweet gesture—and I know I'm just the best mom there has ever been and definitely not a flawed sinner like everyone else!

But I would be a bit offended if my son Winchester took a note I wrote him for his lunch and edited it to be a love note to his girlfriend. The love note wasn't intended for that. It loses all its sweetness and depth if it can be given to someone or something else. It would also communicate to me that my love notes are not treasured. This is because they were reused for a different purpose.

Similarly, the Bible was written for us with particular intent. God's Word was written with specific, clear commands that are to be read as such. It was also written with rich literary metaphors and poems that shouldn't be confused with the commands. The Bible was written in a historical context, referencing specific cultural aspects of those historical moments, but that doesn't mean it isn't applicable to our lives today. It just means that we need to use wisdom. We can't treat the Bible like a social media feed, reposting what we want, maybe adding a pithy comment, and scrolling past the rest.

We ought to be faithful to our reading of the Bible to the best of our reasonable abilities. I struggle with this often, because I have a seemingly never-ending amount of resources to use in my library. It is also my job to do research and teach, so I should have amounts of time to do the best job possible. At least that's true in theory. I easily feel hesitant to post any Bible study online because there is always more I could have read or researched. It seems like there's always more that could be done, but faithfully living to Jesus is asking, "What is a faithful stewardship of my time, resources, and abilities today?" (Life hack: Read that statement again. This applies to *every* area of our lives.)

The Power of the Reread

Start small when you're reading the Bible. Read it slowly. This allows you to see more in the text and prevents eyes-glazed-over skim reading. If we believe that the Bible is the Word of God, why would we skim over it and not really read it? Just to check the box of doing a Bible study? May we never fall into that trap. That's exactly what the Enemy would want us to do—tell ourselves we've accomplished something if we skim-read a passage. He doesn't want us to read the text and have it change our everything. The Enemy knows how powerful God's Word is. Ephesians 6 tells us that the Word is our sword for battle. Of course the Enemy will try to distract us and make our minds wander when we sit down to study our Bibles. So stay alert—this is a battlefield. Also, the Word of God Almighty is powerful, life giving, and life changing, and we must treat it as such.

When my husband was taking his pastoral seminary classes, he had a professor who suggested that his students read a passage twenty-five times before ever beginning to type up a sermon on it. The professor then explained that as the students researched it, prayed through it, and studied it, by the time they stand behind the pulpit they should have read it somewhere around one hundred times. This is a testimony to the power of a reread. Every time I read a text, I notice something new, especially if I read it in a different translation. If you are studying a text, you ought to read it multiple times. If you don't, you're probably not really studying it.

If you are not reading the Bible at all right now, start in the Gospels. I recommend that people read the four gospels once a year because they are like a refresh button for our faith.

They are firsthand accounts of what Jesus said, did, taught, and commanded—and we should cling tightly to them. The whole Bible hinges on Jesus: The Old Testament pointed forward to our need for him, and the rest of the New Testament unpacks the "So what now?" because of him. While I did address earlier that the Gospels build off the Old Testament, I also know that sometimes we need to be met with truth. For me, the Gospels are the perfect refresh button in my Bible study.

My Favorite Bible Study Tool

If you are already immersed in regular deep Bible study, I suggest adding a Bible dictionary to your routine. This tool will immediately enhance your Bible study if you use it. As with a regular dictionary, you can look up any noun and find a Bible-wide definition of it.[1] Most Bible dictionaries are similar to each other—don't worry about finding a perfect one; just start with one.[2] Be warned, however: If you try to use a regular dictionary, it won't have the same effect. Bible dictionaries are worth the investment.

Let's say that during your Bible reading you come across a person, place, or thing that you're not familiar with. If you look it up in a Bible dictionary, you will find what it means in the Old Testament and also in the New Testament. This is

---

1. Remember, this is what we referred to as biblical theology—looking at not just what Paul or Moses says about a topic but what the whole of Scripture says regarding that person, place, or thing.

2. That's the Enemy discouraging you, telling you that you need the perfect Bible dictionary. Most are equally good. Eventually, after time spent using them, you'll navigate toward using your favorites because of their illustrations, entry lengths, and so on. Just start with one and you can add more later if you want to.

powerful, because often I look up a place or item in the Old Testament and find that Jesus interacted with it in the New Testament. I have tons of videos on my YouTube channel sharing how I use Bible dictionaries, but it's not rocket science. Just get one and use it as often as you can. It will enhance your Scripture reading by leaps and bounds. Most Bible dictionaries are equal in value and depth of information, but some will have more pictures or longer entries than others. Ideally, keep one nearby while you're reading your Bible, and every time you come across something you're not 100 percent confident you understand, look up the Bible dictionary entry on that topic. Then as you learn new information that enhances the way you understand the passage, write that down in your Bible (more on this later in the chapter).

The Pastor's Favorite Bible Study Tool

If you are ready to go even deeper in your Bible studies and get line-by-line guidance through the Bible from a trained scholar, then a Bible commentary is what you are looking for. I want to acknowledge that there are some Christians who warn against using commentaries because they don't want you to read what someone else says about the text and just run with it. Some also view the use of commentaries as "lazy," because they can become a crutch that you can't study the Bible without.

But I would rather you walk with a crutch than not walk at all. I would rather you finally understand Jeremiah than never read it at all. I would rather the church as a whole read a bad commentary during their Bible studies than not read the Bible at all. (Remember, God is sovereign to work in, through, and despite everything.)

I do believe that people can benefit more from commentaries than be harmed by them. Notice I used the plural there. *Commentaries.*

I am a big proponent of using multiple commentaries. I want to read the more liberal scholars and compare them against the more conservative scholars. I don't agree with one of my favorite commentaries all the time, but I love it because it always challenges me. Nancy L. deClaissé-Walford has forever shaped the way I see the Psalms, and I now notice slight repetitions or themes in the text thanks to her.[3] But I skim over her constant mentions of "the Hebrew text being corrupt here" or an ascribed historical situation being "added later" because of my tight hold to the text I have before me. Meanwhile, more conservative commentaries, such as the *ESV Expository Commentary*, sometimes run too far in another direction, so I find balance in reading these commentaries together.

Beginners will not want to start with long, expensive commentary sets. I recommend starting with a beginner's Bible commentary, such as the *Wiersbe Bible Commentary* or, my favorite for beginners, the *Bible Knowledge Commentary*.[4] You typically can tell whether it's a beginner's Bible commentary by the length. If it covers the whole Bible and it is about the same

---

3. Nancy L. deClaissé-Walford, Rolf A. Jacobson, and Beth LaNeel Tanner, *The Book of Psalms*, New International Commentary on the Old Testament (Grand Rapids, MI: Eerdmans, 2014).

4. I say *favorite* loosely. Many people like Wiersbe more, but I think the pastors I listened to when I was growing up must have used him too much, because when I read him, I don't find anything new. Therefore, I don't find him helpful. Obviously, this is all up to personal opinion and experience with the text. Just grab a beginner's commentary and start studying!

length as the Bible itself, it will not give you an overwhelming amount of information and typically has been written for a student of the Bible, not a scholar. Use these commentaries as tools to summarize what is going on in the text and to check yourself, making sure that you're not missing anything important.

Commentaries are all organized differently, but for the most part you can expect to find a basic order: introductory text about the book or section of Scripture (depending on how it's been divided) followed by a verse-by-verse or line-by-line exegesis. The texts in commentaries often start explaining the book by giving background information (this stuff is gold), then each paragraph or section (depending on how it is formatted) will start with the verse numbers and then follow with the commentary on the verse. Here is an example for John 4:

Faithy's Commentary on John 4

John continues the narrative seemingly connecting the interaction with Nicodemus and testimony of John the Baptist to the content in chapter 4. Readers note the transition from Judea to Galilee as a telling theme for John— location is growing more and more important to the narrative and patterns of self-revelation in Jesus' teaching.

vv. 1–4. Notice Jesus "must" pass through Samaria. There was no chance Jesus would miss arguably one of the most important conversations he would have in this gospel. Jews didn't go to Samaria. Samaritans were multiethnic people whom the Jews viewed as unclean. First-century readers would not expect Jesus to *have to* stop by Samaria. No good Jew would. But Jesus is not interested in the worldly understandings of being a good Jew. Jesus is after hearts.

v. 6. Jesus arrives at Jacob's well and the reader is reminded about the events that happened to Jacob at a well. Jacob's wife's first "interview" was at a well. Jacob was the undeserving trickster whom God worked in, through, and despite, for his good purposes. Jesus is ready to meet and work through someone unexpected.

Note also Jesus' humanity highlighted in the text. Jesus is thirsty and weary because he is fully human and fully God. This was as important for the first readers as it is for us today. Texts like these form our Christology and tell us Jesus really was who he said he was. He was no vision. He didn't just seem human; he was fully man and fully God.

v. 7. Here enters an unlikely candidate for conversation: a Samaritan woman. Surely if Jesus is the Messiah, he wouldn't spend his time with a defiled woman. In the previous chapter we saw two influential men challenged with the identity of Christ, and yet here, seemingly juxtaposed, is a Samaritan *woman* who, as we will see, also faces the issue of the identity of Christ.

You can see there is a short intro statement to the section of text, which can be as long and in-depth as the author wants to make it. Then each paragraph after this introductory section contains notes after the verse numbers. This is typically how commentaries are organized.

You can read them word for word or jump to just the verse you need help with. There are some commentaries I reference only a few notes on, and others I've read from cover to cover. As you explore different commentaries and authors, you will form your own preferences.

My husband and I prefer different commentators. I like those who are more literary in their evaluations, and he enjoys authors who lean heavily toward the application of the text, such as James Montgomery Boice. Our individual preferences are reflective of the work we do. I am prepping for a Bible study, and he is working on a sermon. This is also reflective of our natural giftings and weaknesses. I don't typically struggle with applying the text (more on this later), but he has to preach on Sunday for twenty-plus minutes on applying the text, so he will use all the help he can get.

I recommend starting simple with a beginner's commentary and noticing the footnotes or references. If you read something like "Miller notes XYZ," google who that Miller guy is. If you keep reading quotes from a scholar or theologian that you like, use some of his or her works. Start noticing who your pastors cite in their sermons, then look up those theologians and scholars.

But start slowly. Early on I noticed that everyone I liked quoted John Owen. Yet I was thoroughly disappointed and demotivated when I ordered a book from Owen and couldn't understand a single sentence. So give yourself grace and work slowly.

My favorite method to recommend to new Bible Nerds is to get one beginner's Bible commentary. After reading your Bible passage for the day, read what the commentary says about the text, then reread the Bible text for yourself again. It all goes back to the rereading method I mentioned earlier—you will grow so much by the repeated reading with new insights and summaries. Eventually, work up to adding multiple commentaries and reread the text each time between referencing them. Then as you learn new information about the culture or text, write it down in your Bible (more on this later).

The Free Bible Study Tool

If you are stressing out about the financial investment of these book purchases, you will be encouraged to discover that there are free commentaries available online. Matthew Henry's commentary is fully online, though it once was in print and you can still find used volumes of his commentaries everywhere. The Enduring Word commentary series is also available online for free. These beginner's commentaries will help guide you in your studies.

There is also free access to Bible concordances and lexicons online. These are tools for understanding the original Greek and Hebrew words used in the Bible (without necessarily having to know much Greek or Hebrew). I prefer Bible Hub, but many also enjoy Blue Letter Bible and Logos (not free). These are resources that show you an interlinear Bible, where the English translation is lined up alongside the original Greek and Hebrew. (The Old Testament was written in Hebrew and the New Testament was written in Greek, with a few exceptions.) These resources also give us the *Strong's* reference number for each word, which is a priceless tool. It's like a phone number for that word in the Bible—you can see everywhere else that word has been used in the Bible and how else it was translated. Remember, just because something is translated as the same word in English doesn't mean it is the same word in the original Greek or Hebrew.[5] The inverse is true as well.[6] So you can easily

---

5. For example, see how Psalm 65 uses *joy* in verses 8, 12, and 13 in the ESV translation. All three verses portray creation as praising God in joy, and the ESV translates all three verses as *joy*, which may tempt us to assume they are all the same word. But this is not true. Synonyms for *joy* are used, but not the same word.

6. See Ruth's use of שׁוּב (*shuwb*), *Strong's* Hebrew 7725.

check the numbers to see whether it is the same word being repeated. To make it even more complicated, you can look to see whether two similar words come from the same root word.

With these free resources, you can also see the grammar. It is labeled whether something is an imperative (command) or just a suggestion. For example, in Psalm 54 within the first two verses there are four imperative commands from the psalmist David to God.

Save me,
הוֹשִׁיעֵנִי (hō·šî·'ê·nî)
Verb - Hiphil - Imperative - masculine singular | first person common singular
Strong's 3467: To be open, wide, free, to be safe, to free, succor[7]

This lexicon entry gives a breakdown of the Hebrew word in this psalm, which is one of these four imperatives of verses 1–2. The top line is how it can be translated in English. Below that line is the original Hebrew. The third line from the top is the grammatical breakdown where you'll see that this is an "imperative" (command), and below that is the *Strong's* reference number (3467). Following the reference number is a definition of the word across the many uses of this word in the Hebrew Bible.

It is important to note that not all of these definitions can work for this word in all the uses of the word. Hebrew is a dynamic language that is largely affected by context. While here

---

7. "Save me," Psalm 54:1, Hebrew lexicon, Bible Hub, accessed May 6, 2025, https://biblehub.com/psalms/54-1.htm#lexicon.

in Psalm 54 it can mean "save," elsewhere in the Old Testament, as in Psalm 20:9, it can be translated as "victory."

There are also some notable issues in the study of words in the Bible—namely, the differences in language from the Old Testament to the New Testament. Because there are two different languages, many use the Septuagint[8] to study words across the Old and New Testaments. The Septuagint is the Greek translation of the Hebrew Old Testament Masoretic Bible. Therefore, if you study the Greek Septuagint alongside the Greek New Testament, it is all one language, and you can see word patterns and usage. The only issue with this is that the Septuagint is a translation, so some nuance from the original can be lost. But the New Testament quotes the Septuagint more than it does the Hebrew Masoretic. This is all an issue to be aware of. Neither is "wrong" to use, but it adds some nuance to the way we study words to know how they were translated into Greek or when the New Testament authors quoted the Septuagint or Hebrew.

I can imagine that as I type this, chugging my coffee on a Monday morning (and struggling right alongside you), you might be feeling confused about this topic of the Septuagint or overwhelmed by the idea of a *Strong's* number. But there are times when these things will make a significant difference in your Bible studies. I also respect you. Maybe nobody has ever told you this, but I believe you *can* study the biblical languages and deepen your understanding of the Bible. We don't have to keep pretending that the serious Bible study club is only for the elites and brainiacs. Friend, if you grew up as a millennial like

---

8. Also referred to as the LXX, the Septuagint was the Greek translation for first-century Greek-speaking Jews of the Masoretic Hebrew Bible (Old Testament).

me, we were writing website code just for funsies back in our Myspace days. We are only as limited as the limits we allow around us. If you want to study the Bible like a pastor or scholar, do it! Because if we really believe God's Word is true, we will treat it like it is and be faithful to it.

And on that note, let's talk about some of the information you will learn along the way.

Taking Notes in Your Bible

Writing what you learn in your Bible is often misunderstood as adding to your Bible or even dishonoring it. But students through all of time have learned by consuming information, processing it, and writing it down. There is a special process that happens in my intellectual growth when I read something, realize it is valuable, then reword it in my notes. On top of that, the information is now recorded there for future me to relearn and build from! That is the value in taking Bible study notes.

Many people don't like that I write in my Bible. They ask why I don't use a Bible study journal for my notes, or they wonder when I will "finish filling up" my current Bible. Both of these questions show me they misunderstand my intention. I want to take notes in my personal Bible that I read and take to church because I want to reference these notes in the future. I can attest to how valuable they are. If they weren't valuable, why would I write them down in the first place?

I take notes right in my Bible because I don't want to miss them the next time I look at that section. The information I have recorded enhances my understanding of the text, and I always want to be faithful to the reading of God's Word. I could record it in a journal, but my journal doesn't go with me everywhere like my Bible does. Besides, journals can get lost or filled up. I have so many prayer journals tucked away in boxes and closets that I could not possibly quickly reference something in them.

The only note-taking system that stays organized, easy to access, and preserved through time is the system I've worked out in my Bible. My notes are right there, in the text, reminding future me that the word used here is XYZ and means such and such. I have notes about how the cultural background enhances the reading and thus the application of the text. I have everything right there in my Bible, and, if necessary, I could teach an entire lesson on a passage using solely my Bible notes. (Actually, I do that regularly.)

I often get asked, "But what happens when you fill up your Bible?" The simple answer is I don't want to fill up my Bible! I want to keep as much room as possible available for future notes. Therefore, I add paper. I write small, and I write only what is necessary. If I can, I will cover up old notes and rewrite them smaller. This is because if I run out of room, I will have to add paper and then that slowly thickens the spine of my Bible. So it isn't about filling up the Bible at all. It's about making the most of the space given. This means that at times I will rewrite notes smaller or cover up older unnecessary notes. Ultimately, it's not about earthly things, such as filling up the Bible with notes or adding my own thoughts. It's about being faithful to the text and building off years of study and acquiring more knowledge.

The power of taking notes in my Bible is in the rephrasing of what a resource said so my brain can process the information and start thinking like these scholars do. It's also in writing notes down in the Bible I read every day so I can reread them for years to come. I take such valuable notes that I want them to go with me everywhere my Bible goes. I don't want to read Isaiah 40 without the priceless notes about the exile, or Hebrews 5 without the notes on Christ as our new High Priest. I take notes in my Bible so they're waiting there in the text for me the next time I study it. I can't read the words without seeing a highlight and an arrow to a paragraph breaking down that specific Greek word or the historical context of a high priest and how Israel understood the role of a high priest. I don't have to spend my time rediscovering Isaiah 40—instead, I get to pick up where I left off in my studies in Isaiah 40.

Context

I like to take notes on context, meaning, and application. My notes can break down the context of a book of the Bible (1 and 2 Kings were written before the exile, and 1 and 2 Chronicles were written after it) or the context of a passage of Scripture (Hebrews 4:14–16 starts and summarizes the second part of the book of Hebrews, which argues that Jesus is the great High Priest). I also include notes on the original historical context, such as the first-century understanding of a mustard seed (see Matt. 17:20) or salt (see Matt. 5:13). Context studies can also be done on a word-by-word level: Is there a word that is repeated in this section of Scripture? In this book? In the Bible overall?

Remember my discussion in chapter 1 about taking a Bible verse like Philippians 4:13 out of context? You might have wondered, "Is that really so bad? After all, who doesn't want to have that cute mug with Philippians 4:13 printed on it?" Context isn't important just because we are trying to be politically correct with the text. Context is important because we want to be faithful to the text (and not misuse it), but also because it adds so much depth.

I already took a jab at Philippians 4:13, so let's talk a bit more about it. We've seen this verse plastered on T-shirts, bracelets, prayer cards, and more. But does the verse really mean you will win the state championships or succeed at every dream you've ever had? Is that what Paul meant when he penned those words to the church at Philippi, that God would help them conquer their opponents and reach all their goals? Absolutely not. Paul was in the middle of a long discourse about enduring through trials. He was writing to believers at a church borne out of suffering and conflict that we first read about in Acts 16.

His focus all throughout the letter is that in the face of persecution and horrible, life-threatening trials the believers could look at the example of Christ's sufferings and have hope because of the cross. They could endure because they were "in Christ" (a phrase he repeats throughout the book). He even says the famous "to live is Christ and to die is gain" statement to really nail this idea home (1:21). Then we reach chapter 4, where Paul is giving final exhortations, encouragements, and instruction. He tells the church to lay their anxieties before God and God's peace will rule their hearts and minds. He encourages them to dwell on what is true, noble, right, and pure. Then he addresses their concern for him in prison. He expresses that he is content in Christ in prison, saying in verse 11, "I have learned to be content whatever the circumstances." Then he expresses that he can do all this through Christ who strengthens him. This is the true context of Philippians 4:13.

With this passage and others like it, we should honor Scripture for what it really says if we are going to claim it has any authority. We need to honor Scripture for what it really says if we want anything more than a self-serving, light reading of the Bible. We must honor Scripture for what it really says if we are going to seek the Lord faithfully every day, not just during the championship season.

Meaning

I also like to take notes on the meaning of a passage. Sometimes I write a summary or outline of the passage so I can better understand the tricky wordage, or I write down quotes from commentaries that do the same. Next to Psalm 145:21 I have a note that reads, "This psalm starts with David's call to worship, goes to community worship, and ends with verse 21 crescendo of worship!" This note helps me understand the movement in the psalm and what the message of the psalm is, so I can then understand why the language changes. From there I can discern how to apply it to my life. In Isaiah 54:1, I have a summary statement written in my Bible that reads, "I'm bringing salvation now, and you're going to burst into joy! I'm bringing you from darkness to light! Death to life! Redemption." While this summary may be confusing to someone else, it helps me not to grow overwhelmed with the lofty language ("Sing, O barren one . . ."[9]) but instead

---

9. ESV.

to feel confident that I *can* understand the text. I understand the promises God is making, and I can see the nature of God at work in Isaiah 54 and that God's Word is still true today.

Notes around meaning can also be notes on specific words. Because of the way translations work, much of the nuanced meaning of an ancient Greek or Hebrew word can get lost in translating it to a flat English word bound by the limits of our cultural English. Literarily speaking, at times there are things like allusions,[10] chiasms,[11] and parallelisms,[12] which inform how we are to understand the meaning of the text. Culturally speaking, meaning can also transform our reading. When we read the word *well*, we may forget that wells were important locations where men often met their wives in the Old Testament. They were also places where God met humankind and provided. We forget that wells were symbols of so much more than a place to quench thirst. They were meeting places, shared among people of different tribes, families, and beliefs. Thus, the meaning of the word *well* is lost when we forget the context and societal meaning behind it. (You can also see how context and meaning are interwoven many times.)

---

10. Allusions are references to previously written parts of the Bible. New Testament authors allude to the Old Testament multiple thousands of times. These are not direct quotes but rather words or phrases that echo, paraphrase, or otherwise refer back to the Old Testament. If I said to you, "Here's looking at you, kid," you might know that's a line from the movie *Casablanca*. First-century readers of Mark 1:7 would recognize the allusion to Exodus 3.

11. A chiasm is a literary device that presents an idea or series of events in a sequence and repeats it in reversed order (or reversed in opposite order). These are found everywhere throughout the Bible, in long and short form. Visually, this presentation makes an X shape, which is why this literary element is called a chiasm, after the Greek letter chi.

12. A parallelism can be synonymous, antithetic, and synthetic. *Synonymous* means the second line of a text repeats the first line in different words. *Antithetic* means the second line is the opposite, contrasting with the first line. *Synthetic* means the next line (or lines) furthers the idea through equal, synonymous phrases.

Application

In addition to notes around context or meaning, I also take notes on application, which refers to how we apply the text to our lives. If we read and study the Bible daily and it doesn't change the way we live, worship, and interact with others, then are we truly studying it? I could argue that if our Bible studies aren't changing the way we live, then we aren't really studying the Bible. But some people think that in-depth study of God's Word directly opposes worshipful application in our lives. They believe that if we are being academic, we could not possibly be worshipful as well.

I'd argue that the academic studies of the Bible fail if they don't enhance our understanding and living out of the text. Few times have academic studies not enhanced my understanding of the text and therefore the application of the text to my life. When we study the regions Jesus traveled to, it is impossible not to view biblical geography differently. We understand that God incarnate traveled those dusty roads with blistered feet and then bent down to clean his fellow travelers' feet. How could this not influence the way I understand the humility God demands of me in serving others?

When studying the ancient Greek and Hebrew words, we should understand the nuance behind the meanings of the words we claim to believe as truth. We also need to understand the concepts, ideas, and feelings the original audience would have had when Jesus spoke those words. Application is so important, but it begins with understanding. So don't be afraid of getting academic—just make sure that it leads to worship.

For example, many have heard great sermons preached on

Isaiah 6. We love the imagery of the angels singing "Holy, holy, holy" and the coal on Isaiah's lips to sanctify and purify his mouth and his mission. But I bet if we were to be honest with ourselves, we wouldn't really feel *close* to the text. That chapter seems too lofty and holy for today's world. We may know it is special, but if you're anything like me, you might wonder what it really has to do with your day-to-day life. You're just trying to make it to your job on time, pay the bills, and survive adulthood. Those angelic words—"Holy, holy, holy"—don't seem applicable to the giant laundry pile we face, do they?

While we know that we can worship through everything and join in with the angels singing, the passage doesn't really seem applicable to our choices in life. But let's look closer. How does this vision come to be? Verse 1 tells us it is in "the year that King Uzziah died." In the Southern Kingdom of Judah (and in the Northern Kingdom too), when a king died, the transition of power usually wasn't as peaceful as it is in our politics today. There was unrest and a lot of uncertainty. The prophet Isaiah had lost the only king he'd ever known. Meanwhile, God's people also had large, scary, powerful Assyria breathing down their necks.

In the midst of this anxiety and unrest, Isaiah gets the vision of the eternal King on the eternal throne. His eyes are pointed toward the heavenly kingdom of God. Do you see how a simple look at context like "the year that King Uzziah died" transforms our understanding of the text? Now it is much easier to apply this to our lives because we see that though we fear the bills and though we are scared of the evil forces that are in power, God always reigns. God rules on the throne even when our paychecks don't cover our expenses. He is the King even when we have a terrible president. God is the eternal King over an eternal heavenly throne though nations crumble and evil seems to reign for the moment. Worshipful application comes from that little bit of context and a mindful understanding of the heart of the text.

I often get my applications from sermons and commentaries, but sometimes they also just come naturally. If you are struggling to apply a text to your life, it probably means you are struggling to understand it. Whether you are reading about the exile, good kings, or a letter to Timothy, all the texts of the Bible serve as stories of wisdom and theology. Every noun, every narrative, every seemingly boring genealogy points to either our need for or our reception of the Savior and his atoning work on the cross.

Remember our Creation, Fall, Redemption, Consummation storyline (fig. 15.1)? Everything that happens along the storyline of the Bible, from Creation to Redemption, points to our need for Jesus and his salvific work on the cross. Everything after Redemption breaks down his work on the cross and the "So what now?" of the cross. It also all looks forward to the final Consummation—heaven.

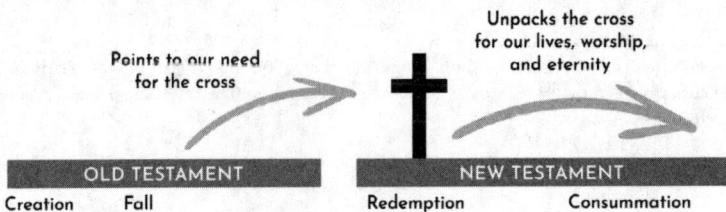

In simple terms, the entire Old Testament eventually points toward our need for a Savior, and the whole New Testament elaborates on this Savior and the "So what now?" of his atoning work. Which means that, if you're tracking with me, the whole Bible centers on Jesus. He is the anchor of the entirety of God's Word. If you're struggling to understand and apply a text to your life, look for Jesus: Is this text showing us a need for a Savior? (Most passages do this in some way or another.) Is the text giving us a type or type scene[13] for something Jesus fulfilled? As with the well analogy I used earlier, I can't read the Isaac and Rebekah,[14] Jacob and Rachel,[15] or Moses and Zipporah[16] narratives without thinking of how Jesus met a Jewish Assyrian[17] Samaritan woman at a well and, instead of betrothal, he offered her the satisfaction she'd sought in her many marriages: himself.

Sometimes the Bible will center on Jesus by explaining what his work means for us today. Look at the many epistles of the New Testament. What they are essentially doing is unpacking how we live because of Jesus now. They tell us how to think about and conceptualize our salvation (that's theology). They also clarify how to worship and live among other believers when there is injustice (Philemon), when you're experiencing persecution (1 Peter), or while you're waiting for Jesus to return (1 Thessalonians 5). Knowing that application can always center

---

13. A type scene in the Bible is a repeated storytelling pattern in which similar events occur in different stories, helping readers recognize key themes (that point to Jesus).

14. Genesis 24.

15. Genesis 29.

16. Exodus 2.

17. In 722 BC the Northern Kingdom of Israel was dragged into Assyrian captivity. During this time many Jewish people intermarried with Assyrians, and this brought forth what we refer to as the Samaritan people. Remember, God's people were not to intermarry with the pagan nations. God's people were set apart as holy! By the time we get to New Testament times (as in the John 4 reference here), Jews viewed these Jewish Assyrian Samaritans as "half-breeds" and wanted nothing to do with them. They would go out of their way to avoid them.

on Jesus doesn't mean that this is the only application, though. Application can also be simple, as in Jonah 1: Don't run from God. Or in Ruth 1: Be faithful and trust God.

But we have to be careful with application. Sometimes application can seem like it is just personalizing the text. We don't need to personalize the text of the Bible and write ourselves into the story. Christ has already done that in his incarnation. Jesus stepped into our lives from the glory of all eternity and was made flesh to walk on our dust and dirt[18] and wipe it from the blinds' eyes.[19] He came from the glory of all eternity to be made flesh and hang on the very tree he wrote the biology for. To be wrapped in the linen cloths he ordained to be woven for his battered flesh. To be buried in a tomb he carved from the earth. God doesn't need us to say, "What does Obadiah mean for my dating life?" No, he has already stepped in, as the literal application, to say: "I am the fulfillment of this." Respond to him. Don't be so focused on the daily right-now application that you miss the big-picture application.

You can go deeper into your Bible studies by using Bible dictionaries, taking notes, and digging into the hard texts of the Bible. But the practical steps we've discussed in this chapter are powerful only when you apply them and practice them. So, friend, don't close this book until you order a Bible dictionary. It's worth the investment, as long as you use it. Keep it with your Bible and use it in your Bible studies. Write down what you learn that enhances the way you read the text, and you will look back in one year and realize you've become a completely different student of the Word. And this happened because you

---

18. Ironically, this is what Adam was made from (see Genesis 2:7).
19. John 9:6.

really believed the Bible is true, you wanted to study it, and you committed to taking the next steps toward understanding and applying it.

Bible Nerd Notes

1. **USE.** Order a Bible dictionary if you haven't done so already (these are available on Amazon, Christianbook.com, or from other booksellers). The next time you are reading your Bible, keep your Bible dictionary open next to you (if it's open, you're statistically more likely to use it than if it's just sitting there closed). Look up every noun (person, place, or thing) you don't feel 100 percent confident you know everything about. Write down what you've learned in a Bible study journal or journaling Bible.

2. **INVESTIGATE.** Pull up Biblehub.com and look up your favorite Bible verse. Take a look at the cross-references, commentaries, and interlinear translations. Next, find the Greek or Hebrew definitions of the most important words in the verse (anything that holds theological meaning). Write down what you learn.

3. **REFLECT.** Revisit what you've written down after steps 1 and 2. What kinds of notes did you write down? Remember our three groupings of notes—application, context, and meaning. Make a mention of what note you found most helpful and why.

CHAPTER 16

This Is Only the Beginning

After my husband and I married in the summer of 2016, we finished our final year of undergrad studies at Covenant College as a young married couple figuring out how to adult. We were both finishing degrees in biblical and theological studies and writing our big final theses. We spent that first year of marriage figuring out how to afford groceries *and* rent as well as trying to find our place in a community of students who were mostly unmarried. I was so focused on marriage, rent, and this new life I had begun that it never hit me that I was finishing my undergrad degree. In fact, I finished my degree a semester early and waited to walk the graduation stage with my husband, so there were a number of months when I was done, but it sure didn't feel like it. By the time graduation arrived, my husband had a job lined up in South Carolina and we'd be moving three days after graduation, so we were also packing up our small apartment. It felt like there was no time to process what it meant to finish my degree and enter the next phase of life.

The morning of graduation, I stood in line to walk the stage with my husband next to me and the nerves racing through my veins (I was terrified I would trip in my cute Payless heels). At this moment, it finally hit me and I realized the gravity of my achievement. Despite coming to college as an individual who was living below the poverty line, despite the fact no other woman in my mother's family had graduated from college, here I stood on the cusp of graduation. And I realized something: If I had learned anything from earning this degree, it was *how little* I knew about the Bible.

If I could summarize the previous four years of studying the Bible and theology, it was that all I had done was taste test a buffet of topics about which I knew only enough to say, "I don't know enough." More than Gunkel, source criticism, or ancient Near East culture, I learned humility. Biblical studies isn't just about memorizing a bunch of Bible verses. It's actually so much better, richer, and deeper. In that moment at graduation I realized I was not done. There was so much more to learn. I still feel that way, even after earning my seminary degree. The studies are never over. The more you learn, the more you realize there is so much more to study—and all of it is really, really good.

The problem you will now face is that the Enemy will try to puff you up, as if you know so much. The Enemy will tell you that you are better than everyone else now that you know about the different types of literature. Often it's silly little things just like that. I see this every day online, in pagans and Christians alike. Someone may read a simple article or hear something new and feel the need to correct or mock others who don't also have this information. But what's interesting is that you almost never see this attitude among scholars. I've found that biblical scholars are the least likely to become petty or prideful about what they know. They know enough to know they know nothing.

My sons are currently in the blessed stage where they are learning to read. Within that stage come spelling tests and phonics lessons, all while they are still wearing Pull-Ups to bed. Last night at dinner, as Winchester was finishing his taco, he snapped at his younger brother, "Well, I know more than you, so you should listen to me!" I always feel a twinge of guilt when he says something like that because I wonder whether that's how Mom and Dad sound when we tell him that Mommy and Daddy know more than he does and are trying to protect him. Little Sutton didn't like his big brother's comment very much, so he shouted back, "That's not true! I know how to spell *orange*, Winnie!" Even though Winchester is older, he hadn't yet learned how to spell *orange*, and I could almost smell the smoke spewing out of his ears. I quickly chimed in that everyone is smart and knowledge isn't a competition before changing the subject. I wonder whether that's how our Father feels at times with his children.

This whole book falls flat if we treat the topic of hermeneutics as anything other than a means of worship. Just like the application of the Bible should lead us to worship, so, too, should the learning of hermeneutics.

We should also be okay with making mistakes, as students—not masters—of the Bible. Years ago I was teaching a Bible study in my college dorm and said, "Paul said this because . . ." probably a thousand times (out of habit because I spent way too much time in the Pauline epistles) before someone finally piped up and said, "You mean Peter?" I was so embarrassed. I am still embarrassed. But why? Why am I blushing while typing this story? We are all just students, and we should celebrate our studenthood because more to learn means more to worship.

Every time we get to crack open our Bibles and learn about a new theological term or location, we have an opportunity to worship our Father and get to know him better. It is not about measuring up or being better, because that's never the point. Jesus is everything for us already.

Sit in Jesus' arms as a student partaking in the glorious worship of the Father. With every new tidbit you learn, remember that there are thousands more things to discover that you don't even know exist yet. With every new Bible study book you finish, forty more were published while you were finishing that one study. You'll never exhaust the depths of the riches of Scripture, and you'll also never exhaust the depths of the riches of worship. Because we serve an infinite God who has made a glorious creation and a rich Word, we will always have more to discover.

Yes, you and I have not even scratched the surface of the riches found in Scripture. No one has. Even the brilliant scholars I read every day haven't gotten close. There's so much more to study about genres in the Bible, literary elements, interpretive issues, and how all of this affects our reading and living out of the text. There's so much I do not know. There is so much the church has yet to spend enough time on. There are scholars upon scholars and books upon books that spend thousands of hours on even the most micro of topics (such as a specific word used in a specific book of the Bible). You and I have the splendid pleasure of humbly acknowledging that what we know about the Bible is only a drop in the bucket compared to the knowledge our grandchildren will have access to. That's why we need to raise the next generation to ask questions like "Why do we understand this verse to mean XYZ?" That's why we need to teach them the difference between hermeneutics and eisegesis.

Just as we stand on the shoulders of the scholars and teachers who came before us and spent their days studying the Dead Sea Scrolls or ancient Near Eastern suzerain treaties, we, too, ought to study and spur on the next generation to carry the baton. Who knows what other scrolls may be discovered or what research may be accomplished to better understand the culture and literature around the Bible. We do this because we believe that the Bible isn't just literature but the authoritative Word of God. We do this because we really believe it is true.

This book doesn't actually end here. You'll set this book aside[1] and then move on to read books written by smarter people.[2] You'll grow daily in your studies of the Word, and one day you'll look back and say, "Wow! I thought Faith's book was good? Ha! She knows nothing!" I know all too well that I have barely scratched the surface of the depths of the beauty of Scripture. Writing this book has made this painfully obvious—on the daily. I write one paragraph, then order a book to read so I can learn more about that topic. But isn't that the student's life?

Studying the Bible isn't doing one in-depth study of the book of Ruth and suddenly having it mastered. To be a student of the Word—or, as I often call myself, a Bible Nerd—is to be someone who knows you can do an in-depth study of Ruth

---

1. But only after recommending this book to ten of your closest friends!
2. Read the books mentioned in my notes! Then read the books in *their* notes. This will take you into a lifetime of deep study and feasting on God's Word.

every month and still find new things in the text.[3] This blessed journey you're on isn't one that's ever finished, really. Even in the Consummation, heaven, we will spend our days feasting on the riches of our God. Our days will be filled in a worshipful discovery of his mercy, love, and truth.[4] So today, as you read and study, you are worshiping in heavenlike discovery of our good God. Let's go read.

---

3. Especially the book of Ruth. I'd argue it's one of the most literarily rich books of the Bible. If you're interested in learning more about literary elements in the Bible, such as parallelism, allusions, and chiasms, check out the courses on my website courses.biblenerdministries.com.

4. For more on his mercy, check out *Strong's* Greek 1656, ἔλεος *(eleos)*, which is used in places like Ephesians 2:4, Matthew 9:13, and Hebrews 4:16. For more on his love, consider *Strong's* Greek 25, ἀγαπάω *(agapaó)*—this is a self-sacrificial love that is unconditional. It is used in places like Mark 10:21, Luke 6:35, Galatians 2:20, and 1 John 4:7. For more on his truth, see *Strong's* Greek 225, ἀλήθεια *(alétheia)*; or *Strong's* Hebrew 571, אֱמֶת *(emeth)*; Jesus is the embodiment of truth. See also John 14:6, Galatians 2:5, and Psalm 119:160.

Acknowledgments

"Thank you" feels far too small. My name may be on the cover, but behind every page are the quiet, faithful efforts of many who gave their time, prayers, and encouragement to make this book possible.

First, my husband, Joseph. This book would not exist without his encouragement, support, and guiding wisdom. Whether it was in a late-night chat about how a chapter should start or end or one of the many much-needed pep talks (I'm a high-maintenance wife, after all), this man was the saint who made it all happen. God has been superbly gracious throughout our lives and relationship, and I see that in your daily grace and support. Thank you for every sacrifice you made through the writing of this book, putting yourself aside to prioritize your wife. I don't deserve such a sweet man as you. You know better than anyone else my total depravity, yet day by day you love and encourage me. Thank you. I love you unceasingly.

Second, to my boys. My sweet boys, you are my whole world. Right now you're too young to care much about this book—you're far more interested in Dog Man and Captain Underpants. But one day, when you hold these pages, even if I'm no longer here, I pray they point you to the greatest treasure of all: a feast in the Word that will never run dry. Jesus is everything you are searching for. But also, Winchester and Sutton, this book wouldn't exist if you didn't: This book was made page by page with y'all in mind. You two make me realize every day how precious life is. This realization is what pushed me to write this book. You also were so patient with me while I took time to step away and write this book. I will forever treasure hearing you (Win) quietly whisper-read the words over my shoulder (I'm so proud of you). I will forever treasure typing up the book with you (Sutt) on my lap in the Asheville airport (you give elite snuggles). Thank you both for being gracious with me and also for cheering me on along the way. I love you beyond measure.

Third, a huge thank-you to my extended family and friends. Grandpaw and Grami for watching the boys as I slipped away during Papa's funeral weekend to finish edits. Patrick, your wisdom and advice throughout the process is a blessing I continue to treasure every day since marrying your son. To my sister Livy, who continued to cheer me on in our late-night chats—thank you. I know our big sister is beaming with pride at the relationship we've built, and somehow you make it hard for me to feel the void she left—because you fill it so beautifully. To all my family—thank you for your prayers and your grace throughout this journey. I know that drawing from a family wound to write this book is tender and difficult for all of us. My prayer is that the fruit of these pages would bring both healing and prevention—for others, and perhaps even for us.

Kyrah, thank you for being not only a friend but also a sister.

You continually remind me of God's grace and truth and that is something I will treasure forever. Andrea Roylston, I cannot fathom a life without your friendship, prayers, and encouragement. Thank you for being such a blessing in my life. To our church family—thank you for being such a wonderful community of believers who have only blessed our family and been a continual example of faithful living. To my pastor, thank you for the advice given in last-minute texts, calls, and sermons. I especially want to thank Lisa and Kathleen, our elders' wives, who faithfully prayed for me and consistently asked about this book's creation. They have been such beautiful examples to me of honest, humble living for the Lord.

To my Patreon supporters—you are like family to me. Your monthly generosity, prayers, and encouragement have carried this ministry more than you know. Your steady encouragement has strengthened my courage, deepened my trust in God, and pushed me to work with greater diligence unto Christ. Because of you, this ministry has grown far beyond what I ever imagined. Without you, its impact would be only a shadow of what it is today. You've stood behind the scenes with quiet faithfulness and consistent joy, and none of this would be possible without you. I resonate with Paul's words when he says, "I thank my God every time I remember you . . . because of your partnership in the gospel from the first day until now" (Phil. 1:3–5). Whether you gave quietly or cheered loudly, whether you've supported since the beginning or just joined—I thank God for each of you by name. Your fingerprints are on every page.

A special thanks goes to those who have been not only friends but also scholarly mentors, offering both personal encouragement and professional insight. Dr. Kelly Kapic, thank you for your insight and encouragement. You have been a long-term role model and your advice and encouragement in the writing of this book were priceless. Thank you for the selfless giving of your time to do that. An additional thank-you to all of Covenant College's biblical and theological studies professors; I would not be the student of the Word that I am today without your guidance and education while I studied at Covenant College. Dr. MacDougall, my first hermeneutics professor, thank you for your passion. Dr. Dryden, thank you for your frank humor, which made the Bible come alive for me. Dr. Ward, thank you for pouring into my husband and me, fueling our passion for missions. Dr. Jones, your wisdom and level-headedness inspired me to continue studying past graduation, though I know I'll never have your number of cool points. Dr. Madueme, you prepared me well with your SIP edits way back in 2016. Although I didn't like them then and neither of us knew it, it prepared me well for an editor's critiques, so thank you for that, though at the time I met you with sass. (Sorry for that.) I owe a significant debt of gratitude to Covenant College, whose education laid the foundation for this book and has had a lasting influence on my life and work.

To my seminary, Erskine Theological Seminary, I also owe a special thanks. Your educators also poured into me a fire for the Word. Additionally, your generosity is what made this book happen: I wouldn't have enrolled if you hadn't given my husband a full-ride scholarship. So thank you for the opportunity to manage an education.

I owe a special and long-overdue thank-you to Dr. Daniel B. Wallace, whose life and work inspire me as both a role model and an embodiment of sacrificial living unto our Savior. Your guidance, especially in the development of chapter 2, and your encouragement along the way have meant more than I can express. Thank you for sharing your ministry and wisdom not only with me but also with the Bible Nerd community. Your contributions to the preservation of biblical truth are something not only this generation but the generations of my children and children's children will benefit from. Thank you.

Thank you to educators who inspired me all the way back in high school and are referenced in this book: Kate Stevens and Robert Dorman. This book is inspired by how you made me feel (capable, worthy, and special) and also by the quality education you poured into me. I must also thank Heritage Christian Academy and especially Dr. Ron Taylor. You provided me with a priceless Christian education in one of the darkest seasons of my life. Thank you to all those who raised the red flag and stood up to care for me like family in that season. Most notably, Jodi Benavidez, Tim and Rebeca Carpenter, and the Hochstein family. I am the woman I am today because of your love. Thank you for treating me like family.

To the Christian YouTube community, I owe you all a large thanks. A special thanks to those who are paving the way, such as Allen Parr, who has been a role model and source of encouragement. Thank you for treating me like a sister in the faith. Your work inspires me more than you'll ever know. This thank-you also goes to countless others such as Coffee and Bible Time and Kirby Kelly, who shared encouragement and prayer. Thank you all for being encouraging brothers and sisters in the faith. Thank you for treating our platform not as a competition but as if we are teammates running the race set before us, keeping our eyes set on Jesus (Heb. 12:1–2).

Finally, a large thank-you to the editorial staff and my literary agent. Trinity, thank you for making this book possible. Thank you for being such an encouraging backbone to this whole project, despite my self-doubt. Andrea Palpant, thank you for your editorial wisdom and guidance. Thank you to everyone at Zondervan who played a pivotal role in the production of this book. From cover design to scriptural annotations, you all brought this dream of a book to life, and for that I am forever grateful. I have loved reading Zondervan books for as long as I can remember, so it has been a special honor to be published by the same publishing house that produced many of my favorite reads.

Though there are countless others to thank for their roles in my life, I owe all that I am (and dedicate all my lack) to my faithful Savior. He is so merciful to work in, through, and despite me. If this book helped anyone, in any way, it is because of nothing that I am, but because he can work through the emptiest, unworthiest, and most wayward souls. Any successes in life are due only to his provision and work. May this book and my life always be testimonies of the abundant grace of the Savior who is "the compassionate and gracious God, slow to anger, abounding in love and faithfulness" (Ex. 34:6).

From the Publisher

GREAT BOOKS

ARE EVEN BETTER WHEN THEY'RE SHARED!

Help other readers find this one:

- Post a review at your favorite online bookseller

- Post a picture on a social media account and share why you enjoyed it

- Send a note to a friend who would also love it—or better yet, give them a copy

Thanks for reading!